C000279503

NIDDERDALE
Walks, History and Heritage

John Burnley

Copyright © John S. Burnley, 2000

All Rights Reserved. No part of this publication may be reproduced, stored in a retrieval system, or transmitted in any form or by any means – electronic, mechanical, photocopying, recording, or otherwise – without prior written permission from the publisher or a licence permitting restricted copying issued by the Copyright Licensing Agency, 90 Tottenham Court Road, London W1P 0LA. This book may not be lent, resold, hired out or otherwise disposed of by trade in any form of binding or cover other than that in which it is published, without the prior consent of the publisher.

Published by Sigma Leisure – an imprint of
Sigma Press, 1 South Oak Lane, Wilmslow, Cheshire SK9 6AR, England.

British Library Cataloguing in Publication Data
A CIP record for this book is available from the British Library.

ISBN: 1-85058-715-9

Typesetting and Design by: Sigma Press, Wilmslow, Cheshire.

Cover photograph: Gouthwaite reservoir from Silver Hill
Maps and photographs: John S. Burnley

Printed by: MFP Design and Print

Disclaimer: the information in this book is given in good faith and is believed to be correct at the time of publication. No responsibility is accepted by either the author or publisher for errors or omissions, or for any loss or injury howsoever caused. Only you can judge your own fitness, competence and experience.

Preface

Each of us has places which we hold especially dear. It may be because they are particularly beautiful, or because they evoke special memories and associations. For me it is Nidderdale which fulfils these happy criteria.

For my parents a Sunday afternoon trip to Pateley was a welcome break from the workaday routine and the drabness of the industrial landscape which surrounded our home. They, no doubt, were far more aware than I of the beauty which unfolded as the car topped the rise above Darley, then sped down towards Dacre Banks and Summerbridge. As a child however, I noticed and questioned the similarities between some of the buildings in Summerbridge and Glasshouses to those of my native "Woollen District", and wondered at their strange sounding names.

Finding the answers to these and many other questions is the theme behind this book. Many people, too numerous to mention, have helped me in my quest, but I must give special thanks to Peggy Garnett-Jones of Wilsill, who has shared her immense fund of Nidderdale lore and innumerable cups of tea with me; to Harold Marshall of Greenhow, whose reminiscences of the lead mines brought a past age back to life; to Eilean Burgess, curator of the Nidderdale Museum, for always pointing me in the right direction and last, but by no means least, to my wife Margaret, for her unstinting support and encouragement and who has, I believe, come to love Nidderdale as much as I.

So what follows is really an account of my own personal voyage of discovery. For those content to "tag along" I hope these pages give flavour and some insight into the delights which Nidderdale has to offer.

John Burnley

Contents

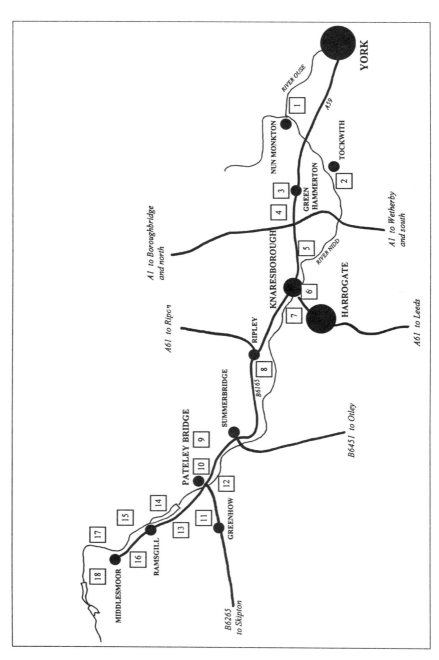

Locations of the walks

The Walks

Introduction

The river Nidd and its valley share many of the characteristics common to all the major dales of North Yorkshire, flowing from the Pennine watershed roughly eastward out onto the Plain of York and there joining the Ouse on its eventual journey to the North Sea.

In many ways however, Nidderdale is unique. Its geology and history have made it so and, being the smallest of the major dales, it exhibits an entity perhaps lacking in its larger neighbours. Do not be misled however, into thinking that this suggests a lack of variety, for this is very far from being the case. A mere fifty-five miles in length, from the slopes of Great Whernside to Nun Monkton, the Nidd Valley nevertheless displays a remarkable variety of landscapes all the more appealing because of their proximity.

Millstone Grit dominates the geology of the upper dale and gives rise to the broad heather-clad moorland which separates it from its neighbours. For much of the year a dreary expanse of pale greens and brown, but for a couple of months at the end of summer, transformed into a vast ocean of purple, stretching as far as the eye can see. Into this moorland the Nidd has carved a deep valley, the sides of which, steepened by glacial action, rise above a flat, narrow floor. Differential erosion of the various layers within the gritstones has caused the oddly shaped outcrops which are a feature at Brimham and other places along the high valley sides.

Carboniferous Limestone makes only a limited appearance in Nidderdale, but where it does reach the surface, as at Howstean Gorge for example, its effects are dramatic and are responsible for some of the dale's most sensational natural features.

Out to the east, beyond the confines of the gritstone moorlands, are the gentler contours of the Vale of York. But in crossing onto those the Nidd has one more major obstacle to negotiate and that it does in grand manner. The great gorge through the Magnesian Limestone escarpment at Knaresborough is the river's final masterpiece before loosing itself in the anonymous waters of the Ouse.

There is beauty all the way here and for some it was a surprise and disappointment that Nidderdale was not included within the confines of the Yorkshire Dales National Park when it was first constituted back in 1954. In some respects this omission may have set Nidderdale at a disadvantage and now perhaps even more so as pressure on our countryside increases. It is timely, therefore, that 1994 marked the year when much of the upper dale was officially recognised as an AONB – Area of Outstanding Natural Beauty.

One

The Flat Lands

It is beside the charming and most unusual village of Nun Monkton that the Nidd finally yields up its identity to the Ouse. There is something exciting about the confluence of one river with another for it is both beginning and end, a point at which decisions have to be made and of course an excellent place at which to start an exploration.

Fenland this area once was and fen-like it may still often appear. Harry Speight, the historian, came here at the height of the great October flood of 1892, when the water was some twenty feet above normal and the river channel was transformed into a raging torrent more than four hundred yards wide. The flood gauge beside the old ferry landing shows what can happen here, though thankfully inundations like those of 1892 are very rare.

The Nidd at Nun Monkton

I like Nun Monkton best on quiet winter days, when the river laps the bank tops and ducks chase and squabble around the trunks of the partly submerged trees, down by the old ferry landing. Through the trees, which line the opposite bank of the Ouse, glimpses of Benningborough Hall can just be seen and beyond that the lofty spire of Newton church.

Nun Monkton is approached from the York to Harrogate road, by way of a long lane, which leads directly onto the huge village green, dominated by an impressively tall maypole. Every feature about this village is unusual, for many of the houses have an elegance which seems somewhat out of place in this rustic setting. The pub too is unusual, at least the name is. Its called the "Alice Hawthorne" and was named, not after some local beauty, but after a racehorse of the Victorian era, whose exploits on the Knavesmire at York caused it to become something of a local legend. The record of her successful career may be found adorning the pub walls even yet.

In Victorian times steamers used to ply between York and Nun Monkton and the village became a desirable place for water-borne commuters. It was also a mecca for weekend trippers, who made their way in droves, up the cobbled ferry landing to play, relax and picnic on the ample village green. The steamers and the ferry are now long gone, but in summer the river bank is often lined with pleasure craft, a colourful reminder of busier times.

It is a delightful stroll from village green to ferry landing, by way of a beautiful tree-lined avenue which leads up to the church. The Early English architecture of St Mary's is almost hidden from view by a huge weeping beech, which in autumn casts down a carpet of gold upon which the visitor must tread to gain access.

In keeping with what we have come to expect from Nun Monkton, the interior of this little church is as surprising as it is beautiful. The present building dates from the middle of the 12th century, but as a site of Christian devotion it goes back much further. Tradition has it that this was the site of a Saxon hermitage, which was destroyed by the Danes in 867AD. The little hermitage was responsible for the Monkton part of the settlement's name, for the nuns were to come later, when in 1153AD, William de Arches and

4

his wife, Ivetta, founded a Benedictine priory here and installed their daughter, Matilda, as first prioress.

Some two hundred and fifty years later this supposedly holy place seems to have gained a somewhat unsavoury reputation. In 1394 the then prioress, Margaret Fairfax, was charged with allowing her nuns to go about improperly dressed and she, herself, was accused of "undue intimacy with certain clergy and other male gentry". Matters were, no doubt, swiftly put to rights, but barely a hundred and fifty years later, on February 8th 1536, the priory was closed, yet another victim of the Dissolution.

What remains of the priory now lies under the manor house, which stands adjacent to the church. It was built by the Paylor family sometime around 1678 and the gardens were adorned by a number of exquisite, life-sized lead statues. These have recently been restored and some of them may be glimpsed from the gate, if you are lucky enough to find it open. What however is not on public view is a most curiously carved stone, depicting in relief, a series of scenes, apparently showing members of the Paylor family as soldiers, farmers, clergymen and hunters. It is said to have been carved by a Dutchman, Andrew Karne, who along with a number of his fellow countrymen, were employed to drain the surrounding marshlands.

Today Nun Monkton is one of the few places in Yorkshire which continues to make much of the traditional May Day celebrations, when the sixty-five feet high maypole comes into its own. However, until the middle years of the last century, the village was the scene of a much stranger ritual, held to mark St Peter's Day, June 29th. Each year, on the Saturday morning previous to the 29th, the young men of the village would go in procession to the foot of an old sycamore tree, which stood close by the maypole, and from there disinter a wooden effigy of St Peter. This act being referred to as "Rising Peter". The effigy then remained on show until the 29th, when it was reinterred, so called "Bury-in-Peter". Just as to what this ritual was really meant to depict has been lost in the mists of time, though of course parading the effigies of saints was at one time a common practice and remains so to this day in certain countries of Southern Europe and Latin America. Was this a rare survival of such a celebration, or could it have been an echo of a darker and more distant past, of Druidism and human sacrifice? Who knows?

Across the river from Nun Monkton lies the equally remote settlement of Moor Monkton. This long street village has little of the charm of its neighbour, but is very popular with anglers and caravaners. A little way downstream is the Red House and, whilst not strictly speaking on the Nidd, no mention of Moor Monkton, nor indeed of the history of Nidderdale, can be complete without reference to this one-time home of the Slingsby family.

The house was built sometime around 1607, but as it stands today is probably only half its original size. There has been much piecemeal and unsympathetic alteration, so architecturally it now has little to recommend it. In warm red brick it is however pleasant enough and a delightful spot to house a preparatory school, the function which it now serves.

The chapel, which stands alongside, cannot however be so readily dismissed. Built at roughly the same time as the house, it does nothing to belie its age. Despite some recent renovation it looks, feels and smells its age and it remains in daily use by the school. It is a treasure-house of rustic Jacobean oak work and contains a magnificent staircase which was originally made for the house. Elaborately carved, it bears the coats of arms of the Slingsby family and those of their relations and friends. On the half landing is a statue of a

Detail from the carved staircase in
Red House chapel

blackamore, cast in lead by Andrew Karne. It was originally an elaborate candle holder, but the device for affixing the candle is now sadly missing.

The Red House will always be associated with the sad fate of Sir Henry Slingsby, grandson of the builder. A staunch Royalist, he once entertained Charles I here and played an active part in the Civil War. Following the outcome he was declared an enemy of the Commonwealth and forced to go into hiding. He chose to incarcerate himself in his beloved Red House, where his presence was known only to a few trustworthy servants. However, during one of his brief excursions into the garden, he was spotted from across the river. Capture soon followed and he was taken to London where he was executed in 1658. His headless remains lie along with those of other illustrious members of the family, in the Slingsby chapel in Knaresborough parish church.

The Red House finally passed from the Slingsbys in 1916 amidst controversy concerning the legitimacy of the heir to the estate. On the death of his father, who had lived in the United States, Charles Eugene Slingsby was due to inherit. However, the will was contested by his uncle, who argued that the rightful heir had died soon after birth and had been replaced by another baby. The grounds for this accusation lay in an advertisement in the San Francisco Examiner of August 24th 1910: "Wanted for adoption, a new-born infant, *must* be male".

Two

Along The Roman Roads

Being within only a few miles of York, this area is laced by a network of Roman roads and indeed the modern A59, between York and Knaresborough, follows one of them, crossing the Nidd at Skip Bridge. The low-lying and ill-drained land must have presented considerable problems for the early road builders, for when a causeway was first built over the ten miles between here and the city it necessitated the construction of no less than nineteen bridges.

Skip Bridge is a notorious spot. Modern cars travel at speed here and the sharp bend has been the scene of some fatal accidents and the Nidd has claimed a number of lives, when vehicles have gone through the parapet and into the river below.

A coaching inn which once stood by the bridge was the scene of a remarkable party, when, on one day in 1807 the two local parliamentary candidates ran up a bill of £2,300 in entertaining local voters. The winner of the subsequent election would have considered the money well spent and the landlord would no doubt have been happy whatever the outcome.

The A59 bisects the twin villages of Kirk and Green Hammerton. The Hammerton family were once major landowners in the area and at one time could boast of riding between York and the Lancashire border, without setting foot off their own land. However, fame and fortune came to an abrupt end in 1536 when Sir Stephen Hammerton paid the ultimate penalty for his part in the ill-starred Pilgrimage of Grace.

Kirk Hammerton possesses a very pretty little church, which, according to some, is the third oldest in England. Its Saxon origins are certainly very much in evidence, being tall and narrow and having a typically squat, square tower. Saxon churches are rare because they were usually built of timber which has not withstood the ravages of time (and fire). Here however the Saxon builders had access to large quantities of Roman stone and so produced a church built largely of reclaimed materials. The Victorian addition to the church now dwarfs the original, but when viewed from the south much of it, thankfully, remains hidden. Inside the walls are adorned by murals, painted by the Victorian artist, George Ostrehan. Clever use of spot-lighting shows these off to great effect.

A track from the village leads down to the river, to the site of Skewkirk mill and bridge. The old mill is now in a ruinous state and both the bridge and weir are now no more. Not a happy place this, one miller hanged himself here and another was drowned. Across the river, to the south, the land rises gently past Wilstrop wood and up towards the battlefield of Marston Moor. The site marks a major turning point in history, when in July 1644 the Cromwellian army routed the forces of King Charles I. and essentially secured the outcome of the Civil War. The graves of 4000 men who died that day lie between here and the river. As I say, not a happy place.

The Roman road to Aldborough turns north at Green Hammerton which in coaching days was an important staging post, boasting no less than four inns. It's a quieter spot now, by-passed by the modern road. There is a large, pleasant green, made the more remarkable by a fine avenue of elm trees.

There is a way across the fields from Green Hammerton to Whixley, where the footpath conveniently emerges by the pub. In Victorian times Whixley was known as the "cherry" village and renowned for the Cherry Feast, held each year on the first Sunday in August. An event which died out only in the early years of the 20th century. Cherry orchards were first planted

Whixley church clock

here by the monks of St Robert's priory in Knaresborough and by the nineteenth century huge quantities of fruit were being sold, even as far away as London. For a time, the income from the sale of cherries formed part of the parson's stipend:

"Cherry tenths the pastor aquireth,
More than souls that he reclaimeth ..."

Perhaps the friars needed reminding of their true purpose in life:

"While cherries grow in Knaresborough, then Whixley should grow
*   piety,*
For twixt the two, as all agree, there should be some variety.
Ripe cherries may be proper food for luscious, dainty beauty,
But piety, not cherry bloom, should find for friars their duty."

Following the Norman Conquest the manor of Whixley was held, for a time, by the de Bruss family, ancestors of the Scottish king, but for several generations, up until the middle of the eighteenth century it was the home of the Tancreds. They lived in the Elizabethan manor house which stands adjacent to the church. The last of the line was Christopher. A scholar and lawyer of some renown, he was the only son amongst a large family of daughters. This latter fact may have helped account in part for his somewhat eccentric nature and his antipathy towards the female sex. At any rate he remained unmarried throughout his life and left nothing to his family when he died in 1754.

In his will there were several bequests towards the endowment of student scholarships, both at Cambridge and at Lincoln's Inn. The Whixley estate was to be placed in the hands of trustees for the maintenance of "twelve decayed gentlemen", who were to live in the house. To qualify these persons had to be over fifty years of age and to have been involved during their working lives in one or other of the "learned" professions. It would seem that the various inmates became, at times, something of a liability for once it was reported that a group of them were running a public house, whilst another distilled brandy. Eventually it was agreed that the pensioners should live elsewhere and that the house should be let to provide an income.

However, by far the strangest, and for the trustees, the most problematical terms included in Tancred's will, were those concerning the disposal of his own mortal remains. It was directed that in the event of his dying whilst away from Yorkshire, he should be buried where he was. However, if he should die in Yorkshire then his remains should never be interred. As it happened, perverse to the very last, he died at home.

For many years Christopher Tancred's coffin resided in the cellar of the house, but ravages due to dampness caused it to be moved and suspended from the wall of the dining room. If the coffin was moved the bones could be heard to rattle and "to rattle like Tancred's bones" became a popular local saying. It was said that the inmates of the house had great delight in demonstrating this somewhat macabre feature. Eventually the coffin became so decayed that, according to tradition, it was possible to reach inside and touch the hair, some of which was taken away as a grisly memento by visitors. Consequently, the trustees decided, sometime after 1850, to commission the carving of a marble sarcophagus. The coffin was placed in this and the whole thing put to reside in the chapel, where it remained a source of acute embarrassment to the various later occupants of the house. Since then various attempts were made to have the remains removed, but with no avail, until 1905 when the commissioners of the Tancred Charity sold the property, and the sarcophagus was moved into the church. Here it stands today, just by the side of the door. It is to be hoped that Tancred's bones are now finally at rest and, just as he had wished, still above ground.

Much of the older parts of the church were destroyed during massive restoration work, during the nineteenth century, largely as a result of the energy and enterprise of the then vicar, the Reverend William Valentine. His forty-year incumbency also saw a doubling in size of the vicarage, but his plans for a tall new spire had to be abandoned when the architect informed him that the tower and foundations would be unable to take the weight. A new clock was however installed. The plaque below it reads:

"I serve thee here with all my might.
And tell the hours by day and night.
Therefore, example take by me
And serve thy God as I serve thee."

The Rudgate, yet another Roman road, runs south through Whixley to cross the Nidd at Cattal. The present bridge lies just a few yards upstream from the original ford, along the road that leads to Hunsingore and eventually joins the A1 at Walshford Bridge

Hunsingore has a large church, rebuilt in 1867 at the expense of Joseph Dent, Esq. of Ribston Hall. It contains some fine stained glass. However Hunsingore's claim to fame lies in the fact that it was the last village in England to erect public stocks, in 1844, a time when, as a means of punishment, they were rapidly falling into disuse elsewhere. Ostensibly for the correction of unruly local youths, the stock's only occupant was the vicar, who one day admitted to a friend a desire to know what being put into the stocks was like. The friend obligingly locked him in, much to the amusement of his parishioners. Soon after this incident the stocks mysteriously disappeared one dark night. They were pulled from the river in York sometime later.

Hunsingore seems to have had a history of unruly behaviour, for the West Riding Session Roles of 1597 record that Francis Thompson and George Allen of Hunsingore were whipped through the town of Wetherby for "contemptuously disturbing the saying of divine service" in the village church.

During the 1930s a happy accident led to the rediscovery of the long lost tomb of the Goodricke family, who were for a long time lords of the manor – the verger and grave-digger both fell into it!

From opposite the church a lane leads down to the river, past the site of the old manor house which was destroyed during the Civil War. The mill is now a private house, though there is mention of a water mill on this site in 1217. In less remote times the local miller also acted as ferryman. The writer and artist, Edmund Bogg, recounts how he and a companion were refused passage on being mistaken for employees of Bradford Corporation Waterworks, who were at that time engaged on building reservoirs in Nidderdale and, according to the miller, "teckin' all t' watter from mi mill".

The footbridge now provides safer and quicker access to the south bank and thence by footpath into the pretty little village of Cowthorpe. This little settlement was once famed for being the home of, what many regarded, as the largest tree in Europe. A massive oak, it stood just behind the church and in 1842 was declared to

The remains of the Cowthorpe Oak

have a girth of forty-eight feet and a main branch which extended over fifty feet from the trunk. As a tourist attraction the tree was a huge success and it was reported that its acorns had been known to change hands at over a guinea each. Sadly little now remains of this once mighty specimen. Harry Speight, writing in 1904, described it as being in a very sorry state and today only a few bleached bones remain to remind us of former glories. A walk around them does however serve to indicate the once massive proportions of this ancient relic. The village road sign still, rather euphemistically, displays a very large and verdant oak tree and a huge painting of it adorns the wall of the public house. I'll leave you to guess what the pub is called.

Cowthorpe's little church is full of character, though sadly no longer in use, it is cared for and maintained by the Redundant Churches Foundation. The tower is most unusual, being partly supported by buttresses, which meet to form an arch over the recessed window. Inside is a large brass memorial to the founders of the church, Bryan Roucliff and his wife, Joan. It is now broken and incomplete, part of it having been stolen and sold as scrap by a tinker sometime during the middle of the 19th century. The carved Easter Sepulchre is a very rare example and dates from the fifteenth century. The tower houses three bells, one of them being inscribed *"O thou blyssid Trinite, of Bryan Rouclyff haf pyte"*, and is the earliest recorded use of English on a bell in Yorkshire. The bell's other claim to fame, or possible notoriety is that, when a boy, Guy Fawkes, often rang them for services.

Trees were apparently not the only things to grow to gigantic proportions in and around Cowthorpe. In 1749, labourers unearthed the skull of a stag. The antlers were still attached and measured six feet from point to point.

Three

Crusader Country

The huge gothic pile of Allerton Mauleverer is virtually all that remains of the settlement of Allerton, which once bordered the Great North Road hereabouts. Granted to the Mauleverer family soon after the Norman Conquest, the property remained in their hands until 1720. Since then the property has passed through a number of somewhat eccentric hands.

For a short time, up until 1789, it was owned by Frederick Augustus, Duke of York, he of "The Grand Old Duke of York" fame. The popular song of the time commemorates the activities of the Duke and his retinue whilst at Allerton. His Royal Highness certainly spent a considerable amount of money on the place during the short time it was in his possession. From his hill top position the Duke had a commanding view over the Great North Road and of the traffic that passed along it. Reasoning that if he could see the road, he then could also be seen by those upon it, he set his "ten thousand men" to work landscaping the grounds in order to block the view. The hill upon which the folly, known as "The Temple of Victory" stands, is reputed to be where "He marched them up to the top of the hill and marched them down again".

In 1789 the estate was sold to a Colonel Thornton, who renamed it, somewhat ostentatiously, "Thornville Royal". A keen sportsman, it was he who built the elaborate falconry, which stands behind the house. The Colonel's mother was an accomplished horsewoman, at one time even racing on the Knavesmire at York. However Thornton's reign did not last long, for the estate changed hands again in 1805. It was acquired by Lord Charles Stourton (Seventeenth Baron), who, being of the Roman Catholic faith, built a chapel alongside the house. Once again the name was changed, firstly to Stourton Towers, then finally to Allerton Park. In 1848 the Eighteenth Baron pulled down the old house and rebuilt it as it stands today.

Allerton Park

It is a magnificent building and without doubt one of the finest examples of Victorian Gothic domestic architecture in the country, but you only need to look at the roofline to realise what a nightmare such a building must be to maintain. By the time it came up for sale in 1982 the house was in a very poor state of repair. Indeed, it was generally accepted that the house would be demolished. However at that point in stepped the obligatory "rich American" in the shape of Dr Gerald Arthur Rolph, who has to date spent some £10 million on restoring Allerton to its former glory. It now has the status of a Grade I listed building so its future should be secure. The opulent, 70 feet high Great Hall sets the tone for the rest of the house. It is open most Sundays and Bank Holidays. Go and see it.

Allerton's church, with its separate Catholic and Protestant graveyards, is cared for by the Redundant Churches Fund. The present building dates from 1745 and reflects a period during which, in general, very little church building took place, hence the unusual nature of both exterior and interior design. Of special interest are the simple box pews and the two-decker pulpit. Over the central tower arch is a large painting of Moses and Aaron, together with the Ten

The Temple of Victory, Allerton Park

Commandments, whilst below are painted the Lord's Prayer and the Creed. In the north transept are the tombs of the Mauleverer family, together with two unique wooden effigies of armoured knights, which are thought to date from the late thirteenth century. The south transept contains the massive, box-like, tomb of Colonel Thornton's mother, Mary, who died in 1800.

The landscape lying to the west of the A1 (now M status) is pleasant and productive and for many years was dominated by the monastic order of the Knights Templars and later by the Knights Hospitallers, whose power base was the manor of Ribston. The Templars came into possession of the Ribston estates, by way of gift, when in 1217 Robert de Ros gave "to God and the blessed Mary and the bretheren of the Soldiery of the Temple, my manor of Ribston ... and the hamlet of Walesford and the mills in the same hamlet".

Over many years the Order gained considerable wealth from their various estates, but their growing political influence brought them increasingly into conflict with both Church and State. Eventually, amidst a plethora of claims and accusations, including one of acts of profanity being carried out at Ribston, their estates became forfeit and passed into the hands of the Knights of the Order of St John, who held them until the Dissolution.

Ribston Hall and park lie within a great loop of the Nidd, with the Hall on a commanding site overlooking the river. The building is largely the work of Sir Henry Goodricke, Fourth Baronet, who died in 1738. Sir Henry was a keen plantsman, who planted many trees on the estate, including the first larches to be grown in England. His most famous introduction however was the "Ribston Pippin", an apple which at one time was very popular and widely grown. The original was grown from a seed sent to Sir Henry from Normandy sometime around 1709. It survived in the orchard until 1835, when the stump was preserved by being covered with a sheet of lead.

Another notable member of the Goodricke family was John, the astronomer. His achievements were recognised in 1783, when he was awarded the Royal Society's Copley Medal, at the age of only nineteen. An achievement made all the more remarkable since he suffered the disability of deafness. He died only three years later aged twenty-two. In 1836 the estate passed into the hands of the Dent family, who continued the arborecultural tradition by planting a pinetum containing over seventy different species of conifer.

There is a public right of way along the drive, from where good views of both the house and the park may be had. It crosses the river by means of a stately little bridge, then swings to the left to continue through the park. A footpath through the fields above the river leads to Goldsborough.

Goldsborough is an unusual and delightful village, which despite considerable modern developments still retains much of its charm. Like Ribston, there is a strong connection with the Crusades here, through the involvement of the Goldsborough family, many of whom lie in the village church. Their carved tombs are some of the finest in the county.

Goldsborough Hall was built by Sir Richard Hutton during the reign of Elizabeth I. It is a beautiful building, in russet brick, enhanced by the warm cream of local Magnesian Limestone. Large windows impart a lightness and elegance, which must have made it one of the finest country houses of the day. The crest over the main

entrance is that of Daniel Lascelles, whose family came into possession of the estate in 1760. We usually associate the Lascelles with
Harewood, but the Royal connection began at Goldsborough, when,
in 1922 the Princess Royal married Henry Lascelles. Thereafter
Goldsborough was regularly visited by members of the Royal Family
whose presence is commemorated in an avenue of trees which they
planted in 1922. Each tree is labelled with the date and the name of
the royal personage who planted it. The cherry trees, which create a
springtime spectacle in the garden, were a gift from the Emperor of
Japan.

Like so many other once grand houses, Goldsborough Hall is now
a retirement home. Few others can however boast such a lovely setting.

Four

Knaresborough and Harrogate

Knaresborough and Harrogate are two of the finest towns in England. That they lie in Nidderdale is a bonus. Close neighbours and inexorably linked, both geographically and historically, they nevertheless are quite different in character. Knaresborough is one of England's oldest market towns, whilst Harrogate is largely a product of the nineteenth and early twentieth centuries.

Harry Speight referred to Knaresborough as the "Coblenz of the Nidd" and, whilst perhaps it lacks something of the grandeur of the German city, there is no denying the impressive views from the castle walls. This must be one of the most sketched and photographed scenes in the whole of England. The town is dominated by the Nidd, whose deep gorge defines its southern limits. In part the river has cut right through the Magnesian Limestone and into the Carboniferous strata beneath. The unconformity, where creamy coloured limestone overlies pink Carboniferous grits may be seen in places along the Waterside, below the castle crag.

Mention of the castle does of course emphasise what a remarkable defensive position had been created by nature and, from the earliest times, man has been keen to exploit it. Knaresborough's potential as a defensive and administrative site was certainly not lost on the Normans, who very quickly set about building a fortress here.

As a bastion against the Scots and sometime rebellious northern barons, it was a favourite with royalty. Both King John and Edward III, spent much time here and enjoyed hunting in the Forest of Knaresborough. Edward gave the castle to his son, the Duke of Lancaster, known as John O' Gaunt, in 1372. It has remained part of the Duchy of Lancaster ever since and so it really belongs to the ruling monarch.

There is not much left of the castle and what there is belies the once great size of the fortress, with its twelve towers and massive keep. Vandalism is certainly no new phenomenon for as early as

1651 a report records that *"the inhabitants of the aforesaid borough and others thereunto adjoining have carried away the best part of the said stones for their own private use"*.

The best-preserved part of the castle is the old courthouse, which is now a museum. A visit here is the best way to gain a flavour of the place before exploring further. It is full of interesting old relics and none more so than the "viameter", the strange wheeled instrument used by John Metcalfe, the blind roadmaker of Knaresborough.

"Blind Jack" is the best known of Knaresborough's many historical characters and his story would have been remarkable even if he had not suffered from such a major disability. Born in 1717, he was blinded by smallpox at the age of six, yet continued to run and play with the other children. By the age of nine he could find his way around the town totally unaided and went on to learn to swim and ride. He was taught to play the fiddle as it was reckoned that this would allow him to earn a living, which for a time he did by entertaining visitors to the hotels in Harrogate. His ability to negotiate the roads and lanes of the district became legend and there is one story of him guiding a traveller from York to Harrogate, by night. On this occasion his companion had no idea of his disability until they reached their destination: "If I had known that I would not have ventured with you for a hundred pounds". "And I, Sir, would not have lost my way for a thousand."

Jack's most singular exploit was to enlist as a musician with the Knaresborough Volunteers at the onset of the Jacobite Rising in 1745 and narrowly missing capture at the battle of Falkirk. Having married, after eloping with the daughter of the owner of the Royal Oak Hotel, in Harrogate, he settled down for a time to the trade of carrier; he thereby learned much of what he was later to put into practice in his most famous occupation as a road builder. His first contract was for three miles of turnpike between Minskip and Ferrensby, on the Harrogate-Boroughbridge road. Many more followed as he gained a reputation for building good roads over difficult terrain. He lived to the ripe old age of ninety-three, dying at his daughter's house at Spofforth on the 27th of April 1810, leaving behind four children, twenty grandchildren and ninety great-grandchildren.

From the museum it is a short stroll to the market square. The town has boasted a market since 1310 and to visit on Wednesday, market day, sees it live up to Leland's description of it as a "quick", that is to say, lively place. Lively certainly characterises Knaresborough, whose narrow streets are often thronged with visitors, from both near and far. Indeed so crowded is the market square, that it is often very difficult to see what it has to offer. The old buildings seem to jostle with each other to gain a frontage onto the square, at the centre of which is a rather pristine looking "market cross. No doubt an original would have stood here at some time, but the present one dates only from 1953, when it replaced a somewhat incongruous electric lamp. What is reputed to be the oldest chemist's shop in England, is to be found here. Its Dickensian bow windows are supported on legs.

A walk along Kirkgate ends, naturally enough, at the parish church of St John Baptist. Mainly fifteenth century, it has a central tower, surmounted by a short spire. It is built, as is much of the town, from Magnesian Limestone and, standing in its recently landscaped surroundings, makes a handsome picture. The clock bears the motto *"Redeeming the Time"*, some of which may be well spent by an inspection of the interior. The Slingsby family memorials are to be found in the chapel off the north aisle. Here lie the remains of poor Sir Henry, who we met earlier at the Red House. The inscription on his tomb describes how he was cruelly beheaded *"by the tyrant Cromwell"*. Also here is Sir Charles, drowned in 1869, when a ferry carrying a party of fox hunters capsized in the river Ure near Newby Hall. The railway station is adjacent to the church. It is now only a halt, but interesting use has been made of the station buildings.

Of the myriad delights which Knaresborough has to offer, many are located down by the river and may be reached from the church by way of the oddly named Water Bag Bank, so called because it was along here that water for the town was carried up from the river in leather bags. If you are in any doubt as to the popularity of Knaresborough come to the High Bridge on a sunny Sunday afternoon or a Bank Holiday. Visitors flock here in droves, some to explore the old town and others to visit the town's oldest and most famous attraction, Mother Shipton's Cave and the Dropping Well.

Knaresborough: the Dropping Well

There is an entrance fee to the Dropping Well estate, but it is well worth the price, especially in autumn, when the near-naked trees allow views of the river and town, not so readily apparent in summer. The estate once belonged to the Slingsby family and it was they who laid out the Long Walk and planted the now massive beech trees which border it. Their glorious leaf colour are an added attraction to an autumnal visit.

The Dropping Well was documented by Leland in 1540 and later described by Speight as "unquestionably the most remarkable petrifying spring known in Britain". Mineral rich water, cascading over a ledge, has built up a tufa screen, below which any object made of absorbent material may be suspended. Within a matter of months such objects are coated and impregnated with lime and thus preserved for posterity. Teddy bears and hats of all shapes and sizes seem to be the prime candidates for the Dropping Well treatment and samples may be viewed and touched at the little museum at the far end of the Long Walk.

Alongside the Dropping Well is Mother Shipton's Cave, where

according to tradition, Knaresborough's famous prophetess was born, in the midst of a great thunder storm, in July 1488. Amongst other things she is credited with the prediction of the motor car, the aeroplane and the telephone, to say nothing of wars, pestilence and famine. Locally she predicted the collapse of the bridges over the Nidd. The viaduct fell down in 1848, during the course of construction. It is to be hoped that its replacement is now safe. Knaresborough just wouldn't be the same without the viaduct. Mother Shipton died in 1561 at the age of seventy-three and is buried at Clifton near York.

Along Abbey Road are some more curiosities, which illustrate yet another feature of the Magnesian Limestone, its softness and the ease with which it may be carved and quarried. The Chapel of Our Lady in the Crag is a totally man-made feature and one of the oldest way-side shrines in England. It was carved by John the Mason in 1408. The figure guarding the entrance is thought to be that of a knight of the Order of the Temple.

Almost directly above the little chapel there is an example of the rock carver's art on an even grander scale. This is the House in the Rock, a dwelling cut out of the rock face and lived in, from its inception, right up to the present day. The work was started by Thomas Hill, a weaver, in 1720 and completed by his son in 1786. As the work progressed it attracted much attention and the younger Thomas became quite a showman, naming the building Fort Montague, dubbing himself "Sir" Thomas and flying a flag from the battlements.

It is a fact that both these buildings are now sadly in need of repair and it says much that both the owners and the local authority have allowed them to decline into such a sorry state. At the time of writing there is, it is hoped, a package being put together by the interested parties which may ensure the future of these two unique attractions.

Nothing remains of the abbey for which Abbey Road is named. Built sometime around the middle of the thirteenth century, it is thought to have stood within the wide sweep of the river, opposite Grimbald Crag. The body of St Robert, its founder, is also lost, but a little way downstream is the site of the hermitage where he spent much of his life. He and his followers worked ceaselessly for the

Moor Monkton, Red House Chapel

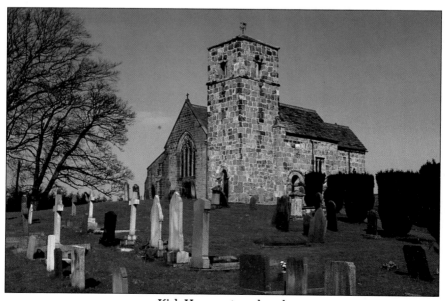

Kirk Hammerton church

Goldsborough Hall

Knaresborough: the river and High Bridge

The Valley Gardens, Harrogate

Braisty Woods

The dale below Pateley

Greenhow

poor and were supported in this by no less a person than King John, a man for whom good publicity seems to have been a somewhat rare commodity. The friars also worked to raise money with which to ransom knights captured by the Saracens during the Crusades, not an insignificant fact considering the whereabouts of John's brother at that time.

Some excavation and restoration work has recently been undertaken at the site of St Robert's hermitage, fortunately without the grisly discoveries that have attended other excavations in this area. It was here that the body of Daniel Clark was discovered, leading to the arrest, trial and eventual execution of Eugene Aram in 1759.

Aram's story is an interesting one, not least because of the controversy that the trial engendered both locally and nationally. To this day opinion remains divided as to his guilt or innocence. Most certainly much of the evidence was circumstantial and perhaps far too much credence was placed upon the testimony of Richard Houseman, Aram's neighbour, who, it was said, was the last person to see Aram and Clark together. Was Aram the poor unworldly scholar, caught helplessly in a web of intrigue or was he a clever schemer dishonestly involved with Houseman and Clark and out to wreak vengeance on the man he thought had betrayed him? Did the two of them argue over Clark's alleged relationship with Aram's wife? Did they come to blows over it? In which case was it murder, or manslaughter or self-defence? After the execution Aram's body was hung in chains close by Grimbald Bridge, from where, as the corpse decayed, his wife collected the bones and gave them a decent burial.

In his defence Aram made much of the fact that human remains are often found in and around historic sites such as Knaresborough. His argument turned out to be sadly prophetic for a hundred years later, in 1853, human skeletons were discovered in a cave by the river, almost directly opposite St Roberts hermitage. The bodies were embedded in clay and were assumed by archaeologists to have been trapped and entombed by a landslide.

The road from Knaresborough crosses the High Bridge, then makes a steady two and a half mile climb, by way of Forest Lane End and Starbeck, to the Stray at High Harrogate. This was once the main way through the Forest of Knaresborough. Though here was no

Yorkshire Sherwood, for the term forest referred not to the natural vegetation but to its status as a royal hunting ground. Indeed most of the area, which extended towards the Washburn valley and as far west as Greenhow Hill, was a bleak upland of heather, gorse and rough grass. Even today, after reclamation and enclosure, it remains a gaunt landscape an area of straight roads, square fields and grey stone walls, somewhere to pass over quickly on the way to friendlier places. The space-age profile at Menwith Hill dominates the skyline with its giant "golf balls" and the only forest is the forest of antennae which surrounds them. So alien to the Nidderdale scene, the least said about it the better.

Four hundred years ago Harrogate itself was part of this waste, probably no more than a small group of cottages, whose inhabitants scratched a bare living from the poor, thin soil. Indeed the very name Harrogate refers not so much to a place, but to a road- Herre-gatte, the Soldier's Way, the way to Herre-law (Harlow), the Soldier's Hill.

Along this way, one day in 1571, rode Mr William Slingsby of Bilton Hall. Stopping to water his horse and perhaps attracted by the flock of lapwings which fluttered around the spring, he discovered that the water here had a most unusual taste. It was similar to that which he himself had sampled in the town of Spa, in the Belgian Ardennes. Quick to realise the potential here, Slingsby had the spring walled around and lost no time in extolling the virtues of its miraculous waters. Thus the Tewit Well, so called after the local name for the lapwing, was the first of over eighty mineral springs to be discovered in the locality.

The number and variety of springs, no two of which are exactly alike in terms of mineral composition, makes Harrogate unique amongst the "spas" of the world. The water which issues from these springs is itself a geological marvel, for this water has never before seen the light of day. It is produced by chemical reaction, deep within the earth's crust and forced up to the surface along cracks and fissures in the overlying rock. The minerals with which it is charged formed the basis of the treatments and cures for which Harrogate became famous, though now, knowing what some of them contain, they would probably be candidates for a government health warning. Indeed not all medical opinion favoured the new "English Spa".

Dr Michael Stanhope referred to Harrogate in his book, "Cures Without Care", as a "rude and barren moore". It was his contention that any good done by the waters was more than offset by the prejudicial effects of the "piercing bleake aire".

Harrogate is indeed noted for its "aire", there's plenty of it and even on calm days the wind always seems to find its way onto the Stray. But a breeze is a small price to pay for that two hundred acres of glorious open space right in the very heart of the town. The Stray is a great arc of green linking High and Low Harrogate. It imparts a feeling of spaciousness and well-being, which makes visiting this town so much of a pleasure. There have been attempts, from time to time, to "do something" with the Stray, but thankfully even the creation of flower beds has been fought off. The original intention was, that following the enclosure of the Forest of Knaresborough in 1778, this area would forever remain open, giving free access to the springs and wells upon which the prosperity of the town relied. The springs and wells are now no more, but the Stray remains. Long may it be so. The only concessions to cultivation are the bright drifts of crocuses, beneath the trees – Harrogate's harbinger of spring.

The developments, which were to make Harrogate into the premier spa town of Europe and England's major inland resort, began in High Harrogate. The Queens Head hotel was built in 1687 and this was quickly followed by the Granby and the Dragon, all within easy reach of the Tewit and St John's wells. The Granby was at one time considered the finest hotel in the town, its wealthy and often titled clientele earning for it the sobriquet "The House of Lords". Not bad for a hostelry which started its life as the "Sinking Ship". The Queens Head, renamed The Queen in 1828, is happily once more an hotel, after serving as the headquarters of the Yorkshire Regional Health Authority for the last fifty years.

If High Harrogate exudes an air of spacious elegance it is in Low Harrogate that it is still possible, to some extent, to savour the delights of the Victorian and Edwardian spa. The Old Sulphur Well, right at its heart, is now the only place in Harrogate where one may still sample the waters, a treat not to be missed, though perhaps not readily repeated. The sulphur water here is reputed to be the strongest in England. I can well believe it! Taking the waters of the sulphur well must, in the early days of its fame, have been a somewhat daunting undertaking, for the place was little better than a morass. Perhaps not surprisingly it soon became the custom for the wealthier amongst those taking the cure to pay local women to carry the water to them at their hotel.

There was money to be made from these waters and, just as in High Harrogate, hotels sprang up to cater for the rapidly growing numbers of visitors. One hotelier, Joseph Thackwray, of the Crown, found himself in trouble when he set about trying

The Old Sulphur Well

to ensure a private supply for his own use. A rival, Mr Jonathan Shutt, of the Swan instigated legal proceedings against him in 1835. The outcome was the setting up of a body of Improvement Commissioners to regulate the use of the waters and the eventual incorporation of Harrogate as a borough. That final act had however to wait until 1884.

The Old Sulphur Well was enclosed in 1842 and called the Royal Pump Room. Now extended, it houses a museum depicting the growth of the town. Opposite are the gates to the Valley Gardens, Harrogate's crowning glory. Sheltered at all times they are a blaze of colour from spring right through to autumn. To sit in the shade of the colonnade, or, in inclement weather, in the newly renovated sun pavilion, is to step back in time and get a real sense of Harrogate as it used to be.

The Valley Gardens occupy an area previously and very aptly named the Bogs and are quite a little hydrological miracle in themselves. Here arose thirty-six of the eighty or so springs discovered in the town. There is a plaque showing the location of all the springs together with an analysis of the chemical make up of their waters. No two are exactly alike. It makes interesting reading!

From here the waters were led off to the various treatment centres in the vicinity, including the Royal Baths Hospital, the tower of which can be seen rising above the trees at the top of the gardens. This centre for hydrotherapy was founded in 1824, by subscription and rebuilt and extended in 1889. The buildings have recently been converted into apartments and housing now occupies the once extensive grounds.

By the late nineteenth century Harrogate was firmly established as the leading centre for hydropathic medicine and when the Royal Baths Assembly Rooms were opened in 1897 they were hailed as the most advanced centre for hydrotherapy in the world. Therapy which included such bizarre treatments as immersion in hot mud and peat are now out of fashion, though the Turkish bath suite is still in operation. The mahogany cubicles and dark green tiling remains, just as it was in its Edwardian heyday, but the entrance is now through a seedy little side door, instead of the grand main entrance. It is a pity, for the Royal Baths Assembly Rooms are a delight. Perhaps more than any other they encapsulates the flavour of times now gone for ever. A refurbishment plan is however in operation, which will involve demolishing the less than appealing 1937 extension and its replacement with something more in keeping with the spirit of the original. We can look forward to the building regaining its position in the forefront of Harrogate's major attractions. The tourist information bureau is housed here so it makes a good starting point for any exploration of the town.

Diagonally opposite is the Royal Hall, built in 1903. Its original name was the "Kursaal" (literally "Treatment Hall"), a reflection of the influence that the German spa towns had on Harrogate's development. The name can still be seen carved above the entrance, but it was changed to Royal Hall, during the First World War, when naturally everything German fell out of favour. The exterior is ornate, the

29

interior quite sumptuous. Alongside stood the Royal Chalybeate Spa Concert Rooms, with beautiful pleasure gardens behind. These were demolished in 1939 and the space is now occupied by an exhibition hall. It looks like a shed. Towering above all of this is Harrogate's new Conference centre. An imposing building, admirably suited to its role and evidencing the town's belief in its continuing role as the country's leading conference and exhibition venue. It is a pity that it is so out sympathy with the elegant buildings which lie adjacent.

Despite the traffic Parliament Street still maintains something of an Edwardian air, with glass and wrought iron canopies over its tastefully understated shop fronts. This short thoroughfare has the distinction of having been the first in Europe to be lit by gas. Here on the corner of Montpellier Parade stands Betty's Café, another Harrogate institution, where one can again step back in time and be pampered with morning coffee or afternoon tea served by smiling waitresses in crisp white aprons.

Five

By the Banks of The Nidd

A stroll by the banks of the Nidd, in pre-glacial times, would have taken us on a very different route to the one we might follow today, for a journey downstream from Ripley would have ended not at Knaresborough, but at Boroughbridge. The old course of the river was blocked by glacial moraine at the end of the Ice Age, causing a huge lake to build up which extended back up the dale almost as far as Summerbridge. When eventually the lake overflowed, the rushing waters carved out the deep gorge which defines its course to this day.

The gorge is at its most spectacular and is most accessible in Knaresborough. Upstream it is heavily wooded and is a haven for a wide variety of rare plants and animals. It is possible to do a circular

Ripley

walk of the gorge from Knaresborough, passing through the delightful little "olde worlde" hamlet of Old Bilton. Modern Harrogate stands on the skyline – it makes quite a contrast. The route also passes by Bilton Hall, one time home of the discoverer of the first mineral spring, William Slingsby. A beautiful tree lined avenue leads from the gate and there is a wonderful view of Knaresborough to be had from the terrace below the house, which is now a retirement home.

The home of the main branch of the Slingsby family lay across the river in Scriven, where for part of their eight hundred year association with the area, they held the title of hereditary Master Foresters of the Forests and Parks of Knaresborough. Between 1572 and 1761 no less than fifteen Slingsbys represented Knaresborough as Members of Parliament.

Edmund Bogg, writing during the 1890s, described Scriven as having "an old English appearance, and, with its pretty green, presents a picture of quiet and peace". It still does. Scriven Hall is now no more but the "pretty green" remains, as does the magnificent oak tree at its centre. This is one of that distinguished group of arboreal giants which actually has a name. It is known as the Lucombe Oak and is, at the time of writing under the sentence of death. Heavily infested by fungal decay, it has been pronounced unsafe and incurable. Naturally, there has been a great outcry against the impending fate of this imposing landmark. Its future lies in the balance.

Up the road in Nidd, the Trappes family fared somewhat better than the Slingsbys at the end of the Civil War. For whilst Sir Henry Slingsby paid for his allegiance to the Crown with his life, the Trappes eventually regained their confiscated property. The estate remained in the family until 1825, when it was sold to the Bradford industrialist Benjamin Rawson. The Hall is now an hotel, adjacent to which is the parish church, small and pretty and with some interesting stained glass. The church clock strikes every hour and is not very popular with the hotel guests.

Nidd looks like a fairly typical estate village, but the history of this little place goes back a very long way. It was mentioned by Bede as being the site of the synod which re-established Wilfrid to the Archbishopric of York in 675 AD. and which set the seal on the future development of the Roman Catholic faith in the north. During the nineteenth century the village boasted an inn with a most curious name. It was called "The Ass in a Bandbox", apparently a satirical allusion to Napoleon – the ass. The bandbox was the conveyance in which he might endeavour to invade England.

Both Scriven and Nidd may have had their moments in history, but it was in rustic little Scotton that events were to unfold which were to rock the English Establishment to its very foundations. Scotton was where young Guy Fawkes was to grow to manhood and where, under the influence of his stepfather, was to develop the religious fervour which would eventually seal his fate.

Guy Fawkes was born in York in 1570, but following the death of his father his mother remarried a certain Dionis Baynbridge of Scotton Hall, a well known Catholic zealot. Here at Scotton young Guy soon learned to understand the fear and resentment which his friends and neighbours felt for those laws which so sadly oppressed them. It is easy to imagine how, at clandestine meetings, this smouldering resentment might grow into something more. Old men might talk, but younger men, like Fawkes were ready to act. Of the major players in the ill-fated Gunpowder Plot, six of them had local connections - The Nidderdale Six! There was Fawkes himself, caught red-handed in the cellars beneath the Houses of Parliament, Thomas and Robert Winter, nephews of Sir William Ingilby of Ripley; Thomas Percy of Spofforth and John and Christopher Wright, Percy's brothers-in-law.

Following discovery of the plot repercussions ran up and down the dale. The Ingilbys were implicated, as were the Yorkes of Gouthwaite, but no hard evidence could be brought to light. John Ingilby was arrested, but later released. Just how far and how deeply the plot extended we will now never know. On being questioned, Fawkes declared his intention had been to "blow King James all the way back to Scotland". What, if anything, was to happen next? For Guy Fawkes it was torture and agonising death far from the beautiful banks of the Nidd.

The road from Harrogate to Ripon now by-passes Ripley, but it would be a pity to miss this little place and the seemingly oversized car park is evidence enough to suggest that there is much here to attract the visitor.

Ripley is a classic example of an estate village. Small, neat and compact and with the typical integrity of design which we expect of such places. Yet it is unique, for despite its Yorkshire stone and slated roofs, this is not typically a Yorkshire, nor even an English village. Ripley has a distinctly French air. It has a town hall which, somewhat pretentiously, proclaims itself *Hotel de Ville*.

The village owes its present form to the eccentricities of Sir William Arncotts Ingilby, one time lord of the manor. Who, impressed by the architecture of the villages of Alsace-Lorraine, had it rebuilt in 1827. Contemporary accounts suggest that Ripley's housing stock was much in need of renovation at that time, so maybe Sir William decided to make a virtue out of necessity.

Ripley and the Ingilby family have a relationship which goes back much farther than the nineteenth century. Indeed the Ingilbys have been here for over six hundred and fifty years, coming into possession of the estate in or around 1330, when Sir Thomas de Ingilby married Ediline de Ripley. Sir Thomas soon set about putting Ripley on the map and was granted a market charter in 1357. The ferocious looking wild boar on the fountain in the market square reminds us of an act of heroism in which Sir Thomas saved king Edward 111 from attack by a wild boar. Apparently Sir Thomas arrived on the scene and dispatched the animal with one blow. From that day to this the wild boar has been the emblem of the Ingilby family.

The Ingilby fortunes have not however always been as bright as those of the first Sir Thomas, for in later years the Ingilbys seem to have developed the unfortunate knack of supporting the loosing side in the troubles which beset our country. For during the troubled times of the sixteenth and seventeenth centuries, the family chose doggedly to adhere to the Catholic faith, a cause that was to cost them dear. Father Francis Ingilby, brother of the then lord of the manor, was executed in 1586. They were also accused of implication in the Gunpowder Plot of 1605, but despite allegations of Catholic forces drilling in Ripley park, no further evidence could be found to link the family with the conspiracy.

The Ingilby involvement in the Civil War was however much

more apparent. With a family history such as theirs their espousal of the Royalist cause was a forgone conclusion. Whilst the then head of the family maintained a diplomatic low profile during hostilities, two of the female members were much less discrete. Sir William's sister took a much more active role in affairs as her nickname, "Trooper Jane", suggests and his wife entertained Cromwell at gunpoint when he billeted himself upon her following the battle at nearby Marston Moor. Maybe Cromwell was mindful of the uncomfortable night he spent at Ripley, for Sir William did spend some time in prison during the Commonwealth.

Ripley Castle has a wealth of treasures and of course it is a family home, still lived and worked in and the centre of an active and thriving estate. A recent attraction has been the rediscovery of the priest's hole where Father Francis would have spent much of his time. The fact that its whereabouts had been lost for so long says much for the degree of skill involved in its construction.

New attractions have been introduced to encourage visitors. These include craft fairs and traction engine rallies and there is an ongoing redevelopment of the gardens which, during the nineteenth century were the subject of much admiration. The two acre walled garden included a run of glasshouses over one hundred and fifty yards in length. There is an obvious rabbit problem, tackled by the present garden staff with determination and good humour. I wonder if Eugene Aram's father had the same problems when he was gardener here? The park now contains many thousands of spring-flowering bulbs and is home to the national hyacinth collection, so springtime weekends are notoriously busy.

Opposite the castle gates stands the church. It dates from the middle of the fifteenth century and replaced an earlier building which once stood much closer to the river. Architecturally the "new" church is something of a mishmash, as it has been so altered and added to over the years. The whole building was originally much lower than it is at present and, in common with many Yorkshire churches, it underwent a major restoration during the latter part of the nineteenth century. However some interesting features do remain. Two of which, the rood screen and the tomb of Sir Thomas de Ingilby and his wife, were brought from the original church. Rood screens were not much in favour following the Reformation so it is probably much to do with the strong Catholic sentiments of the district that this feature survives.

Another pre-Reformation relic is to be found in the churchyard, the lower part, or pedestal of a cross. This is the remains of what is known as a weeping cross and is an example of a feature now extremely rare in England and unique in Yorkshire. The socket into which the wooden crucifix would have been set is clearly visible on the top, as are the indentations around the base against which worshipers would kneel. It is likely that this particular example was salvaged at the time of the Reformation, from its original roadside situation and brought to the relative safety of the Catholic stronghold of the Ingilbys. Many other such crosses must have been destroyed at the instigation of the reforming clergy who were introduced into the district.

For a truly hands-on historical experience, the east wall of the church exhibits a sobering reminder of the horrors of civil war. Here, at chest height, the wall is pock-marked by a series of thumb sized holes. These are the marks left by stray bullets, fired by Cromwell's troopers as they executed Royalist prisoners, taken after the battle of Marston Moor. Other sacrilegious acts were said to have been carried out, including stabling horses in the church and, to add insult to injury, carved upon the tomb of Sir William Ingilby are the words *"No Pompe nor Pride let God be Honoured"*. No wonder Lady Ingilby saw fit to guard her person and property with a cocked pistol.

From Ripley to Hampsthwaite makes a pleasant walk, by way of Hollybank Lane and Clint. A route which is lined by drifts of bluebells in late spring. Clint was once a more important place than it is now, as is evidenced by the stump of a cross and the stocks by the roadside. They must make a unique feature to have by your garden gate. Clint Hall, now demolished was the home of the Beckwiths, once a prominent family in the dale.

Standing by the river on the wide valley floor, Hampsthwaite church makes a very pleasing picture. The present building dates only from 1901, but both it and the churchyard are a treasury of interesting relics and curios. Here is the grave of Jane Ridsdale, who died in 1828. A grown woman, she was only thirty-one and a half inches tall. Here also lies Amy Woodforde-Finden, composer of the once very popular "Indian Love Lyrics", whose connection with Hampsthwaite was as tenuous as it was sad. Her stepson, Eric, an invalid, lived here for a while, until his death in 1913. When, in 1916, his father, Amy's husband died, it was his wish to be buried alongside his son. Amy followed them to the same resting place in 1919. Her exquisite marble memorial stands inside the church.

The church porch was built at the expense of the Thackray family, who count amongst their ancestors the novelist William Makepeace Thackray and another William Makepeace, who suffered at the stake for his Protestant beliefs and who has the dubious distinction of being Yorkshire's only Protestant martyr. For "mouse hunters" the oak screen, prayer desk and lych-gate are all the work of Robert Thompson of Kilburn.

In times past Hampsthwaite seems to have been singularly unlucky in its choice of clergy, for several of them failed to live up to the standards expected. One incumbent, John le Romeyn, had an illegitimate son, who later went on to become Archbishop of York. But more notorious still was Samuel Sugden, parish priest from 1670 until his death in 1686. In 1682, he was accused of frequenting taverns, of brawling and immorality. It was said that on one occasion he threatened a local tradesman with a knife and on another that he assaulted the wife of one of his parishioners. Pictured in my mind however are the events described by a Mrs Hardcastle of Harrogate, who came upon the reverend Sugden crawling home on hands and knees one night, from the local tavern. Sugden, she claimed, made a most improper suggestion to her, proposing that since "her husband went astray...why not she?". The Sugden legacy seems to have lived on in Hampsthwaite for some time, for apparently in the middle of the nineteenth century the village was notorious locally for cock fighting, dog fighting, gaming and swearing.

Leaving aside these less than savoury aspects of Hampsthwaite's past, the modern village has much to recommend it, not least the large triangular green at its centre and the pack-horse bridge tucked away behind the pub. Hampsthwaite was once a place of importance. A Brigantian settlement, it lay on the Roman road between Ilkley and Aldborough. The ford at which the road crossed the Nidd lay just a couple of hundred yards upstream of the present bridge. There was a market here by 1304, before those at Pateley Bridge or Ripley and a fair was held in July each year, to mark the feast of St Thomas the Martyr, to whom the church is dedicated.

It would be difficult to imagine history coming up with another character the like of "Blind Jack" of Knaresborough and stranger still for such a character to have been born within just a few miles of that town. Yet that is exactly what happened in Hampsthwaite. Peter Barker was born here on the 10th of July 1805 and, like Metcalfe, lost his sight at an early age. Also like Metcalfe he also was set to learn the fiddle and for a time this was how he earned his living. Peter must have known of "Blind Jack", but whether or not Jack's story was an inspiration to him, we do not know. Nevertheless he determined to find himself a proper trade and turned his hand to joinery. The first thing he made was a chair, not the easiest thing even for a sighted craftsman, yet it amazed those who saw it. From then on all manner of pieces issued from his workshop, where the only concession to his disability was a specially made ruler, with raised pins to indicate the measurements. Peter also became adept at mending clocks and even succeeded, where others had failed, in repairing the church clock. He died in 1873.

About a mile upstream from Hampsthwaite and linked to it by way of a footpath along the river, is the village of Birstwith. The church, with its lofty spire, stands high up on the wooded hillside above the village. It makes an imposing picture, though somewhat "un-Nidderdale like" and it is not surprising to learn that it dates only from 1856, when Birstwith became a parish in its own right. It was built largely through the generosity of the Greenwoods of Swarcliffe Hall. This family, who came originally from Keighley, made their money in the textile trade and spent much of it here in Birstwith. The mansion they built is quite palatial and occupies a commanding position high on the hillside. Charlotte Brontë spent several months here as governess to the Greenwood children during the 1840s

The river at Birstwith runs wide and makes a spectacular sight as it cascades over the weir. A short distance upstream is the high-arched New Bridge. On an important pack-horse route, this tall and graceful bridge was built to replace an earlier one in 1822:

*"Up Swincliffe an' doon Swarcliffe
And ower t' New Brig into Hartwith."*

Hartwith-cum-Winsley is a parish of small farms, a monotone patchwork of green fields and grey gritstone walls. Many of the farmhouses here are amongst the oldest in the dale. Built of dark, gritstone, their mullioned windows have looked out upon more than three centuries of Nidderdale history. In them lived families who, in many cases, proved just as permanent. Skaifes, Dowgills and Hardcastles have farmed here for generations. Hardcastle Garth was built in 1666, but the farm was bought by the Hardcastle family in 1547 and a Hardcastle was still farming it in 1851. For many years the Hardcastle family were Quakers and a Quaker burial ground can be seen alongside the old house. Brimham Lodge, another fine house, but unusual in having three storeys, was built in 1661 by Thomas Braithwaite, of Ambleside Hall in Cumbria, whose father bought the manor of Brimham about 1650. Thomas never lived permanently at Brimham, but used the house for occasional visits – probably the first person to have a holiday cottage in Nidderdale.

The house stands on the site of an earlier building which at one time belonged to the abbot of Fountains abbey, the surrounding land being farmed as one of the abbey's dairy granges. There are cruck frames in the upper storey, where grain was originally stored and the lower floors have fine oak panelling and stone fireplaces.

Sadly none of these beautiful old houses are open to the public, but many of them lie alongside public footpaths so may be viewed discretely from fairly close quarters

The little hamlet of Burnt Yates has a church and an inn, but it is the school which is of greatest interest, both architecturally and historically. It was built around 1760 by Rear Admiral Robert Long, a distinguished member of an old established local family. It was his wish that, of the thirty poor pupils who were to be admitted, preference should be given to those bearing the surname Long. Equal opportunity had obviously not yet manifested itself in Nidderdale. Indeed girls were only to be admitted if the required number of boys could not be found and their education was to be restricted to reading, writing, sewing, knitting and spinning.

The origin of the name Burnt Yates is interesting and unusual. The little settlement marks the place where a gate, or "yett" once stood across the Ripon to Pateley road, marking the boundary of the Fountains Abbey estate. The boundary can still be found marked on the Ordnance Survey map as the "Monk Wall" and may be traced from the vicinity of the abbey, down towards the Nidd. As to how the "yett" came to be burnt is open to speculation, but these were troubled times and boundary disputes may, then as now, have led to some act of vandalism.

From Burnt Yates the old road to Pateley "wound its toilsome way over the craggy moor of Brimham". Atop this "craggy moor" lie Brimham Rocks, whose weird and wonderful formations cover an area some sixty acres in extent.

Pennant attributed the outcrops at Brimham to the Flood, Whilst Major Hayman Rooke, writing in 1786, described them as the work of the Druids. The rocks were very popular in Victorian times. A sixpenny fee gained admission and the services of a guide, who would no doubt embellish upon the mystical aura with which the rocks were imbued.

Magic and mystery evaporate however on a sunny Sunday afternoon, when the rocks, now in the care of The National Trust, become a huge adventure playground for the scores of trippers who arrive, merely to enjoy, rather than wonder at the scene before them. It is at times like this that the mundane geological facts as to the origin of these outcrops may be most readily accepted. They are largely the result of wind erosion, acting at the end of the last glaciation, when frost action had shattered the strata laid bare by the ice. The variation in resistance of the different layers of gritstone gives rise to the remarkable shapes we see today. Nevertheless if you go alone to Brimham just as the sun begins to set, or, in the soft light of a misty morning, it will make your spine tingle.

Below Brimham lies Braisty Woods, a verdant contrast to the stark grandeur of the rocks. A network of footpaths thread this woodland, which in spring is filled with wild flowers. The little hamlet of Smelthouses is clustered in the valley of Fell beck. It was here that the monks of Fountains Abbey smelted the lead from their mines on Greenhow Hill. The packhorse trains, carrying the ore, crossed the Nidd just below Low Laithe, at a place still known as Lead Wath.

Brimham Rocks: the "Dancing Bear"

Six

The Industrial Dale

Beyond the Monk Wall the landscape, hitherto quite gentle, begins to change dramatically as the valley sides steepen and, rising to barren moorland, enclose the river ever more tightly within its winding course. The valley of the Nidd has now become Nidderdale, the "Little Switzerland" of England as the Victorian romantics called it.

The "New Line", the modern road between Burnt Yates and Pateley Bridge, avoids the high ground and keeps company with the river and the old railway track along the valley. Here, for one hundred and fifty years, Nidderdale maintained a textile industry where, right up to the end, running water provided the power to work the mills.

William Grainge, Nidderdale's local historian, claimed that Charles Gill of Dacre Banks was the first man in England to develop and use a flax spinning machine, "soon after...1793". It would be nice to think of this little industrial backwater laying claim to such a distinction, but the fact of the matter was that John Marshall and Matthew Murray had a flax spinning mill up and running in Leeds by 1788. Gill's mill at Summerbridge is no longer standing. The site is now occupied by the timber yard, but the mill weir, just a few yards upstream, can sill be seen. The rushing waters here contrast sharply with the tree-lined tranquillity of the river just above it.

The name Summerbridge brings all sorts of pleasant associations to mind, but the facts are more mundane. The village is almost entirely the creation of the nineteenth century, built to house local millworkers. There has however been a bridge here since Monastic times when the flocks and herds belonging to Fountains Abbey were driven over it to and from their summer pastures on the hills between Nidderdale and Wharfedale. A family by the name of Todd had a foundry here, producing machinery, including waterwheels, for the local mills. They also produced kitchen ranges, which graced many a house up and down the dale.

Just along the Pateley road is the industrial village of New York, a settlement which owes its creation almost entirely to just one man, Francis Thorpe. Thorpe was perhaps Nidderdale's answer to Robert Owen. A shrewd businessman and an enlightened employer, he acquired New York mill in 1825. The houses he built for his workers are still there to be seen, and the mill complex is largely as he made it. But more than that, he created at New York a most comprehensive, if somewhat paternalistic system of welfare. He introduced health insurance at two pence a month, ran a shop which supplied goods at wholesale prices and he paid for the education of those children who worked part-time in the mill. Acknowledging the less than sober habits of some of his workers, Thorpe arranged for wages to be paid on a Saturday morning, thus allowing wives to get their hands on the money before it could be spent in the pub. Unusually at that time full wages were also paid for feast days and Christmas. With such conditions on offer it might be thought that workers would flock to New York, yet Thorpe

High Street, Pateley Bridge

often complained of the difficulty of attracting labour. Children and young women were in especial demand for the more intricate parts of the manufacturing process and Thorpe was "often obliged to find employment for the parents, what is not profitable to us ...".

It was the ready availability of male employees which allowed New York mill to continue using manual labour to heckle flax, long after the introduction of heckling machines in 1838. The hot, dusty process, whereby the tow, or short fibres, were separated from the longer ones, was not a job to be envied. New York's hecklers often worked up a tremendous thirst and it was not unknown for them to down tools in the heat of a summer's day and take themselves off to the pub for rest and refreshment, a course of action not entirely encouraged by the management. Heckling machines were not given to such unreasonable behaviour which led to them becoming affectionately referred to as "teetotal hecklers".

Francis Thorpe died in 1854, though the business survived until 1883, when a disastrous flood destroyed a huge stock of yarn on the bleaching green. Thereafter the mill stood empty until 1889 when it reopened for the production of hemp ropes and twine. The new owners, Thomas Gill and Sons of Dacre Banks, replaced the waterwheel with a water turbine, which provided the mill with electricity. New York thus became the first place in the dale to experience the benefits of electric lighting. When "sellotape" put an end to the neatly tied parcel and demand for string declined, the Gills turned to the production of polypropylene ropes. The mill is now converted into an industrial estate and houses a variety of enterprises.

If New York is a monument to Francis Thorpe, then the village of Glasshouses most strongly reflects the power and influence of what was perhaps Nidderdale's greatest industrial dynasty, the Metcalfe family. During the nineteenth century they were indeed a force to be reckoned with. The largest employers in the dale, they had local interests which included brewing, linen manufacture, quarrying and lead mining.

The Metcalfe story really begins in Pateley Bridge, where, in 1773, the newly widowed Elizabeth Smith inherited the George Inn and began brewing ale. In 1779 she married George Metcalfe, a flax dresser and when he died in1798 she and her two sons, John and George, continued the business. Elizabeth would regularly ride to Hull to buy Baltic flax, which they spun, first in Pateley, then at Shaw Mills. In 1835 John and George bought the mill at Glasshouses, where they soon initiated a huge programme of expansion, including the construction of the reservoir and the installation of a large new waterwheel. Typically for the Metcalfes, what might have been a purely functional reservoir, was constructed as a landscape feature, complete with central island. Its opening was accompanied by a celebratory meal for the whole workforce and the event was rounded off with a spectacular firework display.

It was however under the auspices of John's son, George, that both the business and the village of Glasshouses went from strength to strength. He built the school and the chapel and was largely instrumental in bringing the railway to Nidderdale. He undertook to raise half the capital himself and, characteristically, had the required sum within six months. The line to Pateley was opened in 1862.

It was George who built the mansion at Castlesteads, on a high promontory overlooking the river, just a few yards upstream of the reservoir. He had long cherished the dream of building here and, in typical Metcalfe fashion, succeeded in securing the property despite considerable opposition, since it lay adjacent to the property of the local squire, John Yorke of Bewerley Hall, who had also expressed an interest. One can imagine the dilemma faced by the owner of the property, Mr Burnaby. If, on the one hand, he sold to Metcalfe, he would risk offending the largest landowner in the dale, whilst on the other, he would alienate a most influential and very wealthy industrialist. He devised a cunning plan. He would offer to sell the property, but at a grossly inflated price, a price which no astute man could accept. Nine hundred pounds was the asking price and sure enough Squire Yorke refused, but to everyone's amazement and, no doubt, to Burnaby's total dismay, George Metcalfe agreed to pay, what was at that time considered to be an astronomical sum. Some impression of poor Burnaby's predicament may be gauged from the fact that he later offered George two hundred pounds to withdraw. No chance! The deal was done and in 1861 work began.

George Metcalfe spent a small fortune on the project and produced what William Grainge described as "one of the most elegant
pieces of architecture in Nidderdale". Though it was, if anything,
slightly restrained and appreciably smaller than Bewerley Hall. It
would however have been surprising if George had not allowed himself a little ostentation. The bridge and carriage drive alongside the
reservoir, was the final finishing touch. Built in Newcastle, the
bridge was carried by rail to Glasshouses, where at the first attempt
to erect it, it fell into the river and had to go back to the manufactur-
ers for repair. By using his bridge George could travel to and from
Castlesteads without the inconvenience and embarrassment of using the lane from Bewerley which ran through Squire Yorkes property. So it was "game, set and match" to George Metcalfe, though
being the kind of man he was, he would derive no satisfaction from
the knowledge that, whilst Castlesteads still stands today, Bewerley
Hall is no more.

Glasshouse mill is now the centre of a little industrial estate. I'm
not sure that the Metcalfes would have approved of all the enterprises carried on here today. Just what staunch Methodists would
have thought of a wine-making company is open to debate, though
they might well remember that the founder of the firm started out by
brewing beer in the back room of the George Inn. The massive un-
dershot waterwheel which once graced the building adjacent to the
winery, is now restored and in working order at Quarry Bank Mill at
Styal in Cheshire. What an attraction it would have been if still in
situ in Glasshouses.

Glasshouses is another unusual Nidderdale name, and once
again down to the monks of Fountains Abbey, who had a glassworks
here at one time. Locally quarried silica sandstone provided the raw
material.

In my memory Pateley has always been popular, for Sunday after-
noons would always find the little park, by the bridge, crowded with
trippers, as youngsters, such as myself, made a bee-line to the
swings, slides and roundabouts. In the past the place seemed to have
been somewhat ambivalent in its regard to tourism. For Pateley has
always regarded itself as a working town It is an ancient settlement,
with a market charter which dates from 1320, but most of what we

see is the product of the late nineteenth and early twentieth centuries, when the population was engaged in linen production, quarrying and lead mining. There were two breweries and two railway stations. These industries are now no more and the railway, which since Victorian times, had carried out the products of the dale and brought in trippers by the score, ceased as a passenger service in 1951 and finally closed altogether in 1964. The main station has been converted into flats and stands alongside the car park. It's a handsome building.

Today however Pateley embraces tourism with open arms and it has its own little gems, even if some of them do need seeking out. The High Street is wonderful. Steep and bone-crushingly narrow, it has hardly changed for a hundred years. Metcalfe's brewery, which stood at the top of the street, has been demolished, as have a few buildings at the bottom, but otherwise it remains much as it was in 1892, when a massive flood had water lapping at the steps of the Crown Hotel.

A starting point for any exploration must be the Nidderdale Museum, housed in the old workhouse opposite the church. This is a treasure house of momentoes from the dale's rich and varied past and should not be missed. It is staffed and run by a group of extremely knowledgeable volunteers whose hard work is reflected in the fact that the museum was voted National Heritage Museum of the Year in 1990.

The church is dedicated to St Cuthbert and dates only from 1826, when it was built on hitherto unconsecrated ground at the top of the town. Inside there is a window depicting the coats of arms of the Sees of Canterbury, York and Ripon, reflecting the association of the dale with these three great religious houses. Edward White Benson, Archbishop of Canterbury from 1892 until his death in 1896 was a member of a very old Nidderdale family, which for generations had farmed in the vicinity of Dacre. There are also memorials to various members of the Yorke Family, who at one time owned much of the land in the upper dale.

The original church, St Mary's, is now a ruin, high on the hillside above the town. It's a stiff climb, but worth it if only for the view it offers. It was built during the middle of the thirteenth century. Below the churchyard a footpath, known, not without good reason, as Pan-orama Walk, leads eventually to the little hamlet of Knott. In the op-posite direction it goes back down into Pateley, past a stone-covered spring upon which is carved the following:

"Ill habits gather by unseen degrees
As brooks run rivers, rivers run to seas
The Way to Church."

A pious thought, not borne in mind by the worthy parishioners, who in 1750 threw the visiting Methodist preacher, Thomas Lee, into the river. Methodism did eventually gain a strong foothold in Nidderdale and for a time, during the middle years of the nineteenth century, Rudyard Kipling's grandfather, Joseph, was minister at Pateley. The young Rudyard spent many happy visits here and his sojourn in the town was marked by a plaque, which until recently could be seen on the front of the minister's house, just a few yards up the road from the church.

Another steep climb from the town is to Scot Gate Ash quarry, from where magnificent views, both up and down dale are to be had. This was once the largest quarry in the Nidderdale and was operated by the ubiquitous Metcalfe clan. The rock here is a massive flag-stone, once in great demand for steps and pavings, both in Britain and abroad. Much stone from here found its way to London and was used in the building of both Victoria Station and the National Gal-lery. A rope operated tramway was used to carry stone down from the quarry to the railway in the valley bottom. The remains of the winch gear can still be seen, as can the line of the track and the little bridge which carried it under the Wath road. The desolate quarry is an eerie, echoing place now and is completely overrun by rabbits.

Seven

On Greenhow Hill

Across the bridge, the road from Pateley to Grassington climbs steeply up Greenhow Hill. Even for modern vehicles this is a climb to be reckoned with and for the less powerful and less "sure-footed" motors of yesteryear, negotiating Greenhow, both ascending and descending, was fraught with considerable hazard.

It is less than three miles from Pateley to Greenhow, yet the two places seem to be worlds apart. Eight hundred vertical feet separates the cosy shelter of the valley from the wild and open moorland which surrounds Greenhow. The climb is exhilarating and the views superb, especially in late summer, when the distant tops are suffused with the purple of blooming heather. Many years ago an elderly resident was asked, by a visiting tourist, if he thought it was possible to see America from the top of Greenhow Hill. "Ah can see farther than that", he replied, "sometimes Ah can see t' Moon".

Sometimes however a cold wet mist hangs over Greenhow for days on end. But worst of all is the wind. According to Rudyard Kipling, who knew the place well, Greenhow folk could always be recognised by " the red-apple colour of their nose tips and their blue eyes, driven into pin-pricks by the wind". The late George Boddy, who spent much of his working life on the Hill, used to tell of the wind blowing the very coal from his shovel when he ventured outside to fetch it and how eggs, frying by the fire, would be sucked up the chimney, so strong was the draught.

In this windswept place, trees are a rarity, rare enough to be known by name. One such, the largest in the village was called "Geordie Thaw" and stood by the roadside along Duck Street. He was cut down many years ago, but I have seen a little bit of him, smoothed and polished and with his name proudly carved on.

It may seem odd that anyone might wish to preserve a piece of old tree, but that's the kind of place Greenhow is, a place of fierce loyalties and long memories. Strange though it may seem, not much more than a hundred years ago this was a thriving community, home to over eight hundred people. The pub, called the Miner's Arms, gives the clue as to what once went on here, though relics of the lead mining industry are everywhere to be seen. Greenhow looks as if it has been plagued by a colony of gigantic moles. There are humps and hollows everywhere, marking the lines of those veins which ran close to the surface, whilst underground the whole hill is a maze of shafts and passageways.

No one knows when lead was first won from the rocks hereabouts, but it is my guess that the hill's store of metal was known long before any commercial value was placed upon it. A great mineralised vein outcrops just below the summit of the hill and may be traced in the quarry there. Perhaps crystals, glinting in the morning sunlight first drew people here. For good reason it was given the name Sun Vein.

There is tangible evidence of Roman involvement in lead mining on Greenhow. Two pigs of lead, bearing the inscription IMP. CAES. DOMITIANO AUG COS VIII. and the word BRIG, were found on Heyshaw Moor in 1735. They are dated AD81 and one of them used to be on display in Ripley Castle. It would seem that the Romans probably used Brigantian slave labour in the mines and maybe these two pigs are the Brigantian equivalent of something which "fell off the back of a lorry". If that was the case, then plainly, whoever hid them never got back to reclaim his horde.

Standing above the beck, just behind Low Farside farm, is what is perhaps the strangest of all Greenhow's store of relics. It is known as the Panty Oon Stone, a rectangular block of gritstone, roughly seven feet long and five feet wide, with a large circular depression carved into it. It was probably the basal part of a mill, used to grind ore ready for smelting. A grindstone fitted into it and would have been turned by either horse or human power. During the 1920s excavations around the stone yielded a few fragments of Medieval pottery, which may help to date it to that time when both the abbeys of Fountains and Byland were involved in mining here.

Below the stone, in the beck side, is the now almost completely silted up entrance to the Sam Oon level, a low tunnel which leads back into the hillside. Jackass level, a few hundred yards away, on the side of Gill beck, is of similar age. With medieval tool marks around the entrance it probably represents the earliest real evidence of mining to be found on the hill. I like to think that it was lead crushed here on the Panty Oon Stone in 1365 that eventually found its way, "by high and rocky mountains and by muddy roads", to Windsor, where, according to the Exchequer accounts, it was used to roof the monarch's great new castle.

In those days there was no permanent settlement on Greenhow Hill and a community only began to spring up after 1597, when Stephen (later Sir Stephen) Proctor purchased what was left of the Fountains Abbey estate. Proctor was not the most popular man in Nidderdale, for as a zealous Protestant reformer he was at odds with his neighbours, most of whom still adhered to the Roman Catholic faith. He was soon involved in litigation with the Yorkes and others over mineral rights and, maybe to strengthen his hand, he encouraged settlement on the hill.

Rightly or wrongly my sympathies lie with the beleaguered Catholics of the dale, spied upon and their every move reported to the authorities. This was often nothing more than a minor inconvenience, but potentially it could be very serious. Remember what happened to Francis Ingilby. Of course Proctor may have been a fine upstanding citizen, keen to protect society from the insurgents within its midst. He must have seen the Gunpowder Plot as a vindication of all his greatest fears.

It is certain that neither Stephen Proctor nor his enemies would have derived any satisfaction from knowing the religious leanings of the majority of Greenhow folk. Hard work and adversity bred into them a strong Non-conformist streak. The Methodist chapel, built in 1814, pre-dated the church by almost forty years and was always more popular. The church is however still standing and, at an altitude of over twelve hundred feet, has the distinction of being the highest in England.

By the roadside, near the top of Cockhill Lane and almost opposite the entrance to Coldstones quarry, there is an unmarked grave. This is the final resting place of John Kay, a poor soldier, who collapsed due to exhaustion whilst marching from York to Lancashire. Having failed to revive him his comrades buried him here and marched on. The story became a legend in Greenhow, a frequent topic for discussion in the pub. There were some said it was true and others who said it wasn't, but one day, probably sometime during the 1870s, Thomas Blackah, Will Longthorne and a few others determined to see for themselves. Armed with picks and shovels, the common tools of their mining trade, they set about their grisly task and, sure enough, a skeleton was unearthed. Satisfied they quickly recovered the remains. Blackah was greatly moved by the discovery and set up a stone (long since disappeared) to mark the grave. He was working at that time in Gillfield mine, which ran under the spot where Kay lay buried and it is said that as a mark of respect he carved the outline of a coffin in the roof of the mine, directly below the grave. I have every reason to believe the truth of this story and a few years ago the late Jack MacFarlane, of Leeds University and myself tried to find Blackah's handiwork, but deep water in the mine thwarted our attempts. I'm sure it's there, just as sure as John Kay lies above it. The old miners, when passing by the grave, would, by way of acknowledgement, often utter the phrase, "John Kay, gie 'im a knock" and accompany this with a couple of sharp raps against the kerb with the toe of their boot. I always do the same.

Thomas Blackah was an interesting character, a man of considerable intellect and with a quick and ready wit. Known as the "Nidderdale Poet", he wrote and published many verses in the local dialect and for a time edited a periodical, which he entitled "T' Nidderdale Almanac". As a lead miner however, Blackah was neither particularly adept nor lucky, once almost coming to grief whilst exploring some old abandoned workings alone. In his spare time he knitted socks, which he sold, along with other bits and pieces, from the front room of his cottage. When the mining industry fell into decline he resolved to leave the hill and emigrated to America. The "better life" did not however materialise and he returned, bitterly denouncing the inhumane treatment meted out to would be immigrants by the authorities. After a time spent working as a collier in Durham, he and his family finally settled in Leeds where he died 1895. He is buried in Woodhouse cemetery.

Cockhill Lane leads down into the very heart of the nineteenth century mining ground. Here, beside Brandstone beck were sited two of the largest mines on the hill. Here also lie the ruins of Cockhill smeltmill. During the middle of the nineteenth century the smeltmill and dressing floor alone would have provided work for eighty folk, whilst many more were employed in the adjacent mines. Over this activity would hang a great pall of sulphurous smoke, carried from the mill in a long flue up to a tall chimney on the hill top above.

Even as late as 1960, much of the smeltmill and its associated build-

Greenhow Hill, the portal at Gillfield Mine

ings were still standing, but now very little remains. The gaping portals of Cockhill and Gillfield mines give no clue as to the maze of passageways and workings which lie beyond them. Nor do they hint at the prodigious labour which went into their making. Pick and shovel work and progress at two yards a week when the going was good.

Cockhill is desolate now, for the most part left to its memories and its ghosts. All mines have their ghosts. This is another of Nidderdale's "tingling" places.

Right on the boundary, between Bewerley and Appletreewick.

along the road which leads to Stump Cross Caverns, stands lonely Keld House. Once the site of a lodge, belonging to Fountains Abbey, it was, during mining times, the focus of a little group of cottages, now long since demolished. At Keld House, for a time, lived the Scaifes, a family dominated by their mean and cruel stepmother. It was said that she was responsible, by her harsh and uncaring treatment, for the death of her stepson "Midge" and the anger and indignation of her neighbours eventually drove her and the rest of the family away. Those who have lived in the house since have spoken of strange and unexplained noises, which they attributed to the restless spirit of the poor boy. Even Harald Bruff, who lived at Keld House for many years, admitted to the presence of the "Midge", but no one had ever seen the ghost. However, the outcome of this sad little tale is as strange as it is poignant. In January 1946, Bruff became seriously ill and one day admitted to his wife that at long last he had seen the ghost. "He stood by my side and told me that he was coming with me". Two days later Bruff was dead and nothing has been seen or heard of "Midge" since then.

Eight

Yorke's Country

The dale beyond Pateley is deep and narrow, a pastoral strip of green rising to the moorland above. It's grand walking country and the intimacy of the place means that, within the compass of what might be no more than a stroll, a wide variety of scenery may be experienced. Riverside and woodland provide for quiet enjoyment, but the high ground gives the views, forever changing with the seasons and with the day to day vagaries of the weather.

Dominating any long view in this part of the dale is Gouthwaite reservoir. Man-made it may be, but a more natural looking stretch of water would be hard to find. The forty-foot high dam, which holds back this two miles of water, is all but hidden by the woodland which borders it. The reservoir is a nature reserve and is visited by a wide variety of water fowl. Golden Eagles have been seen overhead on more than one occasion. There is a small car park on the southern side and a couple of viewing platforms are available for those keen to get a better view of the birds.

During the Middle Ages most of the upper dale lay in the hands of Fountains and Byland abbeys and the pattern of settlement and communications strongly reflects the way in which they used the land. Many of the farms here originated as monastic granges, so may have a history stretching back over nearly eight hundred years, from the time when, in 1143 Roger de Mowbray gave Byland abbey certain rights to pasture animals within his "Chase of Nidderdale". Fountains benefited similarly in 1175 and by the end of the century the two abbeys had gained control over virtually all the Mowbray lands in the dale, including the lead ground on Greenhow.

Following the Dissolution of the Monasteries, much of the land hereabouts came into the possession of the Yorke family. It was they who, for nearly four hundred years, were to dominate the huge tract of land between Bewerley and the moorland acres of Stonebeck Up and Stonebeck Down, at the head of the dale.

The Yorkes will always be associated with Bewerley, which, although it was not their first home, was eventually to become their main residence. Bewerley is a pretty little village, clustered at the foot of Ravensgill and overlooked by the massive rock scar of Guisecliffe. During the early nineteenth century, as was the fashion of the time, the then squire had a folly built here. At a time of severe economic depression the workmen were paid a shilling per day and a loaf of bread. So Yorke got his folly and his tenants were saved from the workhouse. Originally it consisted of three arched towers, but one blew down in a gale, hence its local nickname "Two Stoupes". It is a good vantage point for views up and down the dale and the walk along the top of Guisecliffe can be quite breathtaking. From nearby Crocodile Rock it is said to be possible to see York Minster. I have never yet seen it, though whether that is due to poor eye-sight or industrial haze, I am not quite sure.

You can walk up from Bewerley to "Two Stoupes" through Ravensgill woods, which at one time were laid out with paths and seats as an extension to the gardens at Bewerley Hall. Victorian visitors flocked here to see the woods and the waterfalls, when on occasion the grounds were open to the public. William Grainge wrote of Ravensgill in glowing terms, in his "History of Nidderdale", but one might be forgiven for thinking his references were to the Himalayas rather than the Pennines. Grainge wrote of Fishpond Wood, where the monks of Bewerley Grange had their fishponds, but he did not mention the ice-house, buried deep in the cool woodland, which once provided the Yorke family and their guests with tea-time water ices and sorbets. It's still there, but it takes some finding.

Happy and prosperous times there must have been at Bewerley Hall, but the manner in which the family were to leave it was sad indeed. The estate, which had gone through some difficult times during the middle of the nineteenth century, had been brought to a sound and profitable state by Thomas Edward Yorke. He died in 1923 and the property devolved upon his grandson, then still a boy. It then fell upon his mother to run both the Bewerley estate and the Yorke's other property at Halton West in Ribblesdale. Faced with financial problems at Halton she resolved, against sound advice, to sell the Nidderdale estate. The decision baffled, angered and dismayed the family and puzzled estate workers and tenants alike. Even now, when I discuss these events with those few people old enough to remember, they still remain puzzled by the sale. In 1924, during the depth of the post-war depression the huge estate was split up and sold off and Bewerley Hall was torn down. So now, Bewerley is an "estate" village without its "big house". The carriage drive, from the gate by the bridge in Pateley, leads nowhere. The park is left to grazing sheep and caravan rallies, though it does play host to the Nidderdale Show each year in September. I can however let you into a secret. One small part of Bewerley Hall is still standing. I know. I have been inside!

Of course the Cistercian monks were here before the Yorkes. Fountains Abbey actually bought, what amounted to virtually the whole parish of Bewerley, for £100. Not a bad piece of real estate and probably a bargain even at that time. The chapel, once attached to Bewerley grange, is still standing, all but hidden in its surrounding cloak of trees. It was built by Marmaduke Huby, abbot of Fountains, in 1494 and bears the motto of which he was so fond, *"Soli Deo Honor et Gloria"*. At one time the building was used as a school for the children of the local poor, but happily today, after restoration and repair, it again serves its original purpose and is a nice little focal point for the community.

When I first came to know it, during the late 1950s, the Watermill Inn was still a working flax mill. It was then known as Foster Beck Mill and was one of the last mills in the dale still to use its huge water wheel to drive its machinery. It finally closed down in 1967 and, for a while, stood empty. I suppose it was too much to ask that the rustic charm of this little mill might have been retained intact and really one should be grateful that its present use does at least ensure its survival.

Foster beck must be the shortest stream in Nidderdale. It is really just the lowest section of Ashfoldside beck, which suddenly changes its name at the point where it meets with the waters of Brandestone beck. Opposite this confluence stands a large stone building, now surrounded by caravans and proclaiming itself the Heathfield Caravan Park. This is another building which for a long time stood empty and deserted. As a child I explored its dark inte-

Foster Beck Mill

rior, without ever knowing what it was. At that time the crest and initials I Y and the date 1855, above the door, meant nothing to me. The crest is that of the Yorke family and the mill was built by John Yorke, to smelt lead ore from the mines alongside Ashfoldside and Brandestone becks. This mill replaced an earlier one which stood close by and, at the time of its construction, incorporated a number of innovative features, including a water powered fan which, was used to provide a continuous blast of air to the furnace, instead of the traditional and less efficient bellows. Yorke's new mill also used a much more sophisticated fluing arrangement, whereby the exhaust gasses first passed through a water-cooled condenser and then along a stone-built flue, which was one and a quarter miles in length, before finally being emitted from a tall chimney high on Heathfield Rigg. Annual cleaning of the flue was said to recover lead worth up to £800, though what it did to the health of those involved one shudders to think. Part of the flue is still visible in the field behind the caravan park.

Prosperous and Providence mines lie about a mile further up the valley, with the ruins of Prosperous smeltmill alongside the beck. A huge waterwheel was once employed here to drive the pumps which drained the mine. In the beckside, just above the mill, is the low, narrow portal of Yorke level, one of the many adits cut into the hillside along the course of the beck.

The track continues towards Merryfield, once a very productive mining area. The place has the appearance of a lunar landscape. It is eerily quiet now, but the "private" notice on the gate serves as a reminder that, like some ancient volcano, the lead mining industry here is merely dormant. It may not yet be extinct.

For those intrepid enough to venture further the course of the beck leads on to Low and High Stoney Grooves. Remote indeed are these two mines, but there is quite a lot to see at Low Stoney Grooves, including the remains of the engine house and chimney. Also to be seen are the remains of a circular buddle, a kind of centrifuge in which the finest particles of ore could be separated out. It was worked by horse or man power. Its oak-boarded floor is still intact under a protective layer of soil.

If it were not for the large sign, heralding the attractions of the Sportsman's Arms, Wath could easily be missed, for woodland all but obscures the settlement from the road. The best way to approach is from Pateley, by way of Silver Hill and Wath Lane. From this high vantage point the situation of this charming little hamlet may best be appreciated, for it is tucked cosily against the protective wooded hillside, which rises behind. Taking the "high road" to Wath also provides a chance to savour one of the finest views in the dale. From the reservoir a patchwork of green rises to the moorlands above. In the distance the wide shoulders of Great and Little Whernside just nudge the horizon, white-topped in winter and a purple haze in late summer; a kaleidoscope, as scudding clouds cast their ever changing pattern of shadows over the landscape.

Wath stands at the point where a glacial moraine spans the valley floor, constricting it somewhat and in so doing creating an ideal place at which to cross the river. A fact reflected in the very name of the settlement, for wath is the old Norse word for a ford. Ford and bridge stood side by side for many years. Until it was widened late in the nineteenth century, the bridge, being of typical pack-horse design, was not wide enough for wheeled traffic. In times of flood, when it became too dangerous to use the ford, farmers and carriers would often take a wheel off their cart and pull it over the bridge with one axle riding on the parapet.

For a place of its size it is perhaps surprising to learn that Wath once boasted two places of worship, the Protestant Mission church and the Methodist chapel. They ranked as two of the smallest ecclesiastical buildings in England. The chapel is less than twenty-five feet square.

More unlikely still, Wath once had a railway station. Now tastefully converted into a private dwelling, it is the building which stands just by the bridge, opposite the Sportsman's Arms. Wath was one of four stations, the others being at Pateley Bridge, Bouthwaite and Lofthouse, on the course of the Nidd Valley Light Railway. This unique service was owned and operated by Bradford Corporation Waterworks Department who came on the scene with plans to build reservoirs at the dale head. A rapid and reliable means of transport was required to service this undertaking so Bradford Corporation put in an application to build and operate a railway between Pateley and Angram, a distance of thirteen miles. The application was granted with the proviso that the corporation should be obliged to run a passenger service as far as Lofthouse, with stations at the intermediate settlements. The line was opened in 1904, following a report from the Board of Trade inspector which stated that "the line appears in every respect very soundly constructed and the station buildings are exceptionally good for a line of this description. The signalling arrangements are considerably in excess of Board of Trade requirements for light railways". Praise indeed, but only reflecting the sound design and workmanship which characterise all of Bradford's undertakings in the dale. Two second-hand locomotives were purchased from the London Underground, which was at that time converting to electricity. As a minor indulgence they were given the names "Holdsworth" and "Milner", in honour of the chairman and deputy of the Waterworks Committee. Personnel were dressed in uniforms of the finest quality, supplied by the Bradford firm of Brown Muff. The station master at Pateley must have looked quite resplendent in his sixty-five shilling (£3.25) suit. The other three station masters may have felt a little envious, for their suits only cost fifty-eight shillings and sixpence each.

Riding the little train must have been a delightful way to have made the up-dale journey and, despite falling passenger numbers, many people were saddened when the line closed to passenger traffic in 1929. It closed altogether and was dismantled in 1936, when Scar House reservoir was finally completed.

From Wath the road up the dale follows its switchback way along the shore of Gouthwaite reservoir, the first of Bradford's reservoirs to be built in Nidderdale. Work began in 1894 and it was completed in 1901, but this reservoir was not in the original plan. Fierce opposition to the reservoirs had come from both landowners and industrialists in the dale, the former concerned with the possible effects on fishing, whilst the latter feared that a reduced flow would affect the waterwheels which powered so many of the mills. Gouthwaite therefore was to be a compensation reservoir, designed to allow a sufficient flow downstream to maintain the wheels in adequate motion. It fell to the manager of New York mill to liase with the reservoir keeper regarding the rate of flow required.

Whilst the construction of Gouthwaite reservoir no doubt satisfied some, it must have dismayed many others, as some of the best farmland in the upper dale disappeared below its waters. Harry Speight, writing in 1894, just before work began on the dam, described the scene thus:

> *"Beautiful and retired is the dale about Gouthwaite; the green fields with their browsing cattle, the quiet homesteads, each nestling in a grove of trees ..."*

Of Burn Gill he says:

> *"The gill, I am told, is the warmest nook in the valley. In spring, primrose and other wildlings usually open their tender blossoms here before a flower can be found elsewhere"*

And, on the subject of Riddings Gill, someone was once moved to pen the following eulogistic lines:

> *"How sweet it is in Riddings Gill,*
> *To lie upon the grass so still;*
> *With ears alert, with closed eyes,*
> *And listen to the sounds that rise*
> *From babbling brook, from purling pool,*
> *From waterfall and cascade cool."*

There is a petrifying spring deep within the recesses of Riddings Gill. I have seen a sponge which has been given "the treatment", it makes a most unusual garden ornament.

From the historical point of view, the greatest misfortune to have resulted from the construction of Gouthwaite reservoir was the loss of Gouthwaite Hall, a sixteenth century building and one of considerable architectural merit. In this day and age it would, no doubt, be protected by Listed Building status. The Hall's demise was however a lesson which served to show that reservoir building was not always the exact science we might expect. At the initial flooding, residents of the Hall were told that the water level would come no further than the garden gate. When it breached that Mr Barlow, the engineer, reassured them that it would rise no higher than the doorstep. New Gouthwaite Hall stands on the up-slope side of the road! It is a venerable looking building and contains within its fabric much of the original house, which was so quickly dismantled, when it became obvious that the waters of the reservoir were bent on their relentless upward migration.

Gouthwaite was the original Nidderdale home of the Yorke family. It was bought by John, youngest son of Sir Richard Yorke, merchant and one-time Lord Mayor of York. Coincidentally, John's mother was Jane Mauleverer, so here was an early union of what were to become two very important Nidderdale families. A further useful match was made in 1560, when John's grandson, Peter, married Elizabeth, daughter of Sir William Ingilby of Ripley.

Being secure within the fastnesses of their northern estates, the punitive measures, enacted against those of the Catholic faith, were more of an encumbrance rather than a direct threat. So it was until the arrival of our old friend Stephen Proctor, who, following the discovery of the "Gunpowder Plot", stepped up his vendetta against the Yorke-Ingilby clan. In one case, Sir John Yorke was accused of failing to pay the curate at Middlesmoor church, of preventing parishioners from attending church and allowing a piper into the churchyard to "make there with their piping and revelling, such a noyse in times of praier as the mynyster colde not well be hearde".

Proctor's greatest measure of success against the Yorkes came about over what, in this enlightened age, we would consider a very

Middlesmoor in the snow

trivial affair. A band of travelling players had been invited to Gouthwaite to provide some holiday entertainment and, as part of their repertoire, acted out an imaginary dialogue between a Catholic Priest and an Anglican minister. The denouement of this little drama was the carrying off of the minister by the Devil. By some means Proctor came to hear of this and straightway denounced Sir John to the authorities, whereupon he and four of his household were incarcerated in the Fleet prison. Eventually he was charged with bringing the Established Religion into derision and he and his wife were each fined £1000, a high price to pay for half an hour's entertainment.

When the Yorkes finally left the cosy rusticity of Gouthwaite, first for Richmond, and later for Bewerley, the story of the old house continued to be punctuated by periods of fame. In 1730 it was the birthplace of William Craven, famed man of letters and Master of St John's College Cambridge. Some years later Eugene Aram taught school here, before moving on to Knaresborough and notoriety.

The winding road continues up-dale beyond Gouthwaite, closely hugging the side of the reservoir, past farmsteads, some of which have been here since the Cistercians held sway in these parts. Colthouse, by Riddings Gill, was one of the earliest of Byland Abbey's granges, established soon after 1140. Roger de Mowbray gave land here specifically for pasturing eighty mares and their foals. Across the valley is Covill House, one of Fountain's granges and one of the best farm sites in the upper dale. It is thought to be the site of the ancient lost village of Poppleton.

Ramsgill is a picture-postcard village, with its tree-shaded green, pump and ivy-clad inn. The little settlement originated as one of the Byland granges and the remains of the chapel, just one gable wall, are to be seen behind the church. Ramsgill was the centre of the Yorke domain. As lords of the manor this is where they held their manor courts and the Yorke Arms was once their hunting lodge. The present church, built in 1842, was paid for largely through the generosity of the family and the proud trees, bordering the green were planted by the "Old Squire" in 1897, to mark Queen Victoria's Diamond Jubilee.

It is, however, as the birthplace of Eugene Aram that Ramsgill will always be remembered. He was born here in 1704 and his marriage to Anna Spence, of Lofthouse, on May 4th 1731, is recorded in the parish register in Middlesmoor church. However the house in which he lived is no more, swept away in a tide of nineteenth century improvement, along with the other thatched hovels which once made up a less than picturesque community. How times change and what a sought after place Ramsgill is now.

Just beyond the bridge a narrow road leads off to Bouthwaite. It terminates at a gate, from where a track climbs steeply up onto the moor and eventually, at one time, to the abbeys of Fountains and Byland. The land on this side of the valley belonged, as the name Fountains Earth suggests, to Fountains Abbey, but the monks of Byland were allowed to cross it and use the bridge so long as they did not allow their animals to graze "en route". That stipulation was however generously overlooked when flood or foul weather impeded progress.

During the early sixteenth century Bouthwaite Grange was tenanted by a widow, Margaret Brown, and her son. It must have been a productive place, for in 1512 they provided eighty stones of cheese, forty stones of butter and thirty stirks to the abbey. Following the Dissolution Bouthwaite became the property of the Inman family, in whose hands it stayed for several generations. "Bold Robin" Inman is best remembered for slaying four intruders, who one night entered the house intent on robbing him. The club with which he dispatched his attackers, remained a family heirloom until well into the nineteenth century.

The wide moorlands, which "Bold Robin" knew so well, are friendly enough on a bright summer's day and beautiful to behold when the heather is in bloom, but how dank and drear when the mist is down or the rain is falling. To those who travelled them in the past they must have presented a formidable obstacle and the prospect of becoming benighted amongst their rolling expanses, must have been dreadful indeed. Out on Raygill House Moor are the Wig Stones, a group of grotesque gritstone outcrops. Were these the way-markers of the Celts who once trod these parts. or the "witch" stones of our Saxon forebears? In either case these solitary naked rocks must have held some mystical significance.

High on Fountains Earth Moor are two of the weirdest of these stones, Jenny Twigg and her daughter, Tib. Tall and gaunt, they stand in splendid isolation. But who or what was Jenny? Was she "Jenny T' Wigg", Jenny the Witch? In early English folklore the name Janet, or more commonly, Jenny, was often given to a witch, but the origins of our Jenny's name may go back even further. As to who first named Ms. Twigg and her daughter, that is now lost in the mists of time, just like they become lost in the mists which so often swirl around them.

> *"Jenny Twigg and her daughter Tib,*
> *Jenny with her black cat Gibbe;*
> *Jenny Jenny Jenny Dibb,*
> *Long the thread you spin. "*

For centuries Lofthouse was the "end of the road", for there was no way for wheeled vehicles beyond here and the road over the moors to Masham was made fit for motor traffic only as late as the 1950s. Nevertheless late nineteenth century Lofthouse was a much livelier place than it is now, boasting three shoemakers as well as a blacksmith. But these were busy times in this part of the dale. Lead was being extracted at Lolly Scar and Blayshaw and coal was mined close by. Reservoir construction also provided work and brought men here, though Tom Bradley, then landlord of the Crown Hotel, may have had mixed feelings regarding the economic benefits of all this activity. "I've 'ad some does wi' t' navvies. I've 'ad pint pots thrown at me."

There are more sober sentiments to be found inscribed on the fountain-cum-war memorial in the village square:

> *"If you want to be healthy, wealthy and stout,*
> *Use plenty of cold water inside and out;*
> *Let animal and man drink freely."*

And on the reverse:

> *"A pint of cold water three times a day,*
> *Is the surest way to keep the doctor away;*
> *Whosoever thirsteth let him come hither and drink."*

They seem to have had quite a thing about water in Lofthouse, During the great October flood of 1892 it could be seen bubbling up through the fire grate in the Blacksmiths house. The Nidd flows underground through Lofthouse to re-emerge a few hundred yards beyond the village at Nidd Head Springs, opposite the old vicarage.

In the vicinity of Lofthouse Nidderdale's hitherto somewhat prosaic geology takes a much more complex and interesting turn. Hereabouts erosion has revealed the underlying limestone and the beds of both the Nidd and its tributary, How Stean beck, are carved in this extraordinary rock. Above the village the river bed rises like a broad limestone staircase towards what must be one of the prettiest little waterfalls to be found anywhere in the Dales.

For sheer grandeur, however, pride of place must go to How Stean Gorge. Here the beck, plunging from the moorland above, has carved a defile some seventy feet deep and over half a mile in length. Advertised in Victorian times as Yorkshire's "Little Switzerland", it was, like Brimham, a popular attraction to those visitors "Taking the Waters" at Harrogate. Walk-ways and bridges make the gorge a safe and pleasant place to visit and there are the added attractions of caves and passages which may be safely explored. You can hire a torch for that express purpose. Children love it. Tom Taylor's Cave is reputedly named after an outlaw who once used it as his place of refuge, but the cavern is better known as the place where a horde of Roman coins were discovered by Thomas Jackson, a local lad, in 1868. He once described how he came to find and, subsequently, loose one of the coins:

"I was a small boy when I found a small coin. I took it to the school and was showing it to the other boys, when t' maister calls out "What have you got there Tom?" So he maks me tak it up to 'im an' he taks it away. "Oh", says he, looking at it. "I'll tak it to be magnified." An' its been magnifying yet."

The majority of the horde came into the hands of George Metcalfe who gave ten of them to Squire Yorke, in exchange for a pig of lead, excavated during building work at Bewerley Home farm. Maybe George thought that this gesture might in some way go towards mending relations after the Castlesteads debacle and I suppose that the Squire had a reasonable claim on them, after all he was lord of the manor.

As to when the coins were hidden, AD 418 might be a likely date. That was the year when, according to the Anglo-Saxon Chronicle, "the Romans collected up all of the hordes of gold that were in Britain and some they hid in the earth...". Tom Taylor's Cave obviously did not then enjoy the popularity that it does now.

Blayshaw Gill also reflects the geological dichotomy of the area. A fault, running along the gill, reveals the Carboniferous Limestone to the north and the Millstone Grit to the south. From the bridge the two rocks may be compared regarding their resistance to erosion and the differences in vegetation which they support. The limestone, known locally as Blayshaw Marble, was once quarried nearby. The pillars in the abbey church at Fountains originated here.

High on Blayshaw Bents are the remains of old bell pits, worked for iron in the Middle Ages, by the monks of Byland Abbey. One pit was discovered in 1876, when a farm labourer fell into it. It was in a remarkable state of preservation, with ironstone in the base and pick marks still plainly visible on the walls. The viaduct-like structure, which can be seen crossing the hillside, supports the pipe carrying water from Scar House reservoir. Water in the pipe flows under gravity at a rate of four miles per hour and takes eight hours to complete the thirty-two mile distance to Bradford.

Middlesmoor must exert some kind of magnetic attraction. The tight little cluster of buildings on the hill top draws the eye and demands a visit. There is a good road now, but the village doesn't really take kindly to the motor car. Such trappings of the modern age seem out of place here, so for effect I like to walk to Middlesmoor, through the fields from Lofthouse and up the steps by the side of the churchyard. From here there is a wonderful view back down the dale. Middlesmoor was popular with visitors during Victorian times. They must have considered themselves intrepid explorers, to have reached such an isolated place and their comments are recorded for posterity in the visitors book at the Crown Hotel.

The church contains a number of interesting relics, the oldest of which is the Cross of St Chad. It is reckoned to date from the tenth or eleventh century. However, the most surprising feature of this remote little church lies hidden away in the tower. There is a peal of six bells, presented in 1868 in memory of Simon Horner, merchant, philanthropist and native of the village. The inauguration is remembered each year, in June, with the "Bell Festival", which culminates in a huge party for the local children. Mary Ann Barkwith, Simon Horner's great-niece, left a sum of money to pay for this annual treat, but it was on the clear understanding that "no rude games be permitted".

Nine

The Hidden Dale

Beyond Lofthouse the valley of the Nidd takes an abrupt northward turn and in so doing narrows considerably. If, during my childhood, the Nidd Valley Light Railway had still been in existence, I might have wondered where the line went from there, but, as it was, for me, Nidderdale ended at Middlesmoor. It was, I suppose, a reasonable assumption to make. Middlesmoor stood on the top of a hill, from where you could look straight back down the valley and what's more, it was where the tarmacked road ended.

A youthful passion for Ordnance Survey maps was to enlighten me regarding the geography of the dale, but what made these hitherto unexplored upper reaches even more intriguing was the fact that, in order to reach them by car, a permit had to be acquired from Bradford Corporation Waterworks Department. Today access is much easier and visitors are encouraged, though the feelings of anticipation are still there as one drives through the gate and pays the fifty pence toll.

Despite the now open road to Scar, this, like any other part of Nidderdale, is best explored on foot and the way to do that is to take the old route by way of Thrope Lane. Before construction began on the reservoirs there was no valley floor route beyond Lofthouse so wheeled traffic was virtually precluded from here on. The present road merely follows the old track bed of the railway line, a fact which accounts for its gentle curves and steady gradient.

There are delightful views from Thrope Lane, which leads eventually along by Thrope farm. This is a lovely old building, with stone mullioned windows and stands on a site which has been occupied for many hundreds of years. It was originally a grange belonging to Fountains Abbey, as indeed were many of the farms in this part of the dale. The craggy hillside rises steeply above Thrope, up to Dale Edge and the church-like shooting hut which crowns it. Close to, this building is far less impressive than it seems from a distance, but the view from up here is wonderful. For sheer exhilaration, if not for comfort, this is the place to be on a windy day in winter.

From Thrope farm the path drops down to the dry bed of the Nidd, which it follows to Limley. Now just a single farm, Limley was in the past, quite a considerable hamlet. For generations it was the home of a family by the name of Bayne, who claimed descent from Donald Ban, king of Scotland from 1093 to 1099. Walter Bayne, it is said, migrated to Yorkshire in 1182, after some disagreement with the authorities. If that is the case he must surely have been the first of the growing number of "off-comed 'uns" to have made Nidderdale their home.

Goyden Pot, the great hole in the river bed, which swallows up the flow of the Nidd, is just a few yards beyond the farm. This pot hole should really be as great an attraction as Howstean Gorge, but the trouble is that it is unreliable. Except in periods of very wet weather the river sinks almost imperceptibly into its bed about four hundred yards farther upstream at Manchester Hole. When, however, the river is in flood, the sight of the turbulent water pouring down Goyden pot is quite a spectacle. In dry weather it is safe and easy to enter the mouth of the pot hole (but no further) and it is not uncommon to stand at the entrance and hear strange disembodied voices come floating up from the depths below, for the cave is a favourite with potholers.

Rising above Manchester Hole is the steep wooded Hillside of Beggar Moat Scar. This is another misleading name and has nothing to do with either beggars or moats. A more closely correct pronunciation might be "Beckermonds", a term found elsewhere in the Dales and meaning the "meeting of the waters". Here steep slopes and a tight bend in the valley caused severe problems for the railway and hundreds of tons of rock had to be blasted away and a tunnel dug through the hillside.

The dale head is a wild place, dominated now by the great dam of Scar House reservoir and the waters which lie behind. It was, however, not uninhabited, for farms dotted the valley sides as far as Angram, a Norse settlement lying right at the foot of Great Whernside.

When I first visited Scar House reservoir during the summer of

Looking to the dale head from below Rain Stang

1966 the wounds torn in the flesh of the valley sides were still com-
paratively fresh, for barely thirty years had elapsed since the last
workmen left the site. The trees which now hide the dam wall were
mere saplings then and did nothing to lessen the impact of this massive structure, towering over my approach. One hundred and seventy feet high, Scar is the largest stone-built dam in Europe. To be
perfectly correct, the dam is not actually built of stone. It is stone
faced, the interior constructed of that exotically named material
"cyclopean rubble" – large blocks of rock set in concrete.

Thirty years on and things have mellowed somewhat, trees have
grown and scars have healed. I confess that I have mixed feelings
about the place. On the one hand I am saddened at the assault on the
pristine grandeur of the dale head, yet on the other the end product
is in itself almost beautiful. Bradford corporation had enough good
sense and taste to build in stone, won from the hillsides just above
the dam. As the years go by it blends increasingly into the landscape
from which it was hewn. Everything about Scar speaks of quality,
from the beautifully dressed facings on the dam to the stone lined
culverts through which the little rills are directed into the reservoir.
Bradford's city fathers were no doubt very proud of their achievement, for the plaques mounted on the end of the dam wall testify as
much. They must also have delighted in a trip out to survey their
handiwork, for where else but Scar would you find a reservoir
keeper's house complete with a "Committee Room"?

The great dam at Scar was not part of the original plan as envis-
aged by the designers of the waterworks scheme. It was first in-
tended that there should be three smaller reservoirs at the dale head,
namely Angram, Lodge and High Woodale. The latter would have
been on the downstream side of the present dam, but it was discovered that it would not be possible to transfer water by gravity flow
from a reservoir at that height. A higher dam at Scar thus became the
more difficult alternative and was chosen despite considerable opposition. Many members of Bradford City Council considered it an
expensive "white elephant". Time has however proved them wrong
and more recently many towns and cities in England may have
wished to have been so well provided with water supplies as is Bradford.

The logistics required for such an undertaking during the early years of the 20th century and in an area as remote as this, were quite formidable and not least of these was the recruitment and support of a workforce, which, at the height of operations, was some twelve hundred strong. To cater for such a workforce a whole new village was built. With typical Bradford thoroughness, this was no shanty town. There were sixty-five bungalows for the staff and labourers were housed in ten hostels, each presided over by a housekeeper and a staff of three cooks and cleaners. Feeding fifty hungry navvies must have been more than a full-time job, though apparently rabbit pie and stew was often on the menu. Rabbits abounded at Scar then just as they do now.

Those who lived at Scar village, mainly as children then, speak with fond memories of the time they spent there, for this was no frontier existence in the "back of beyond". Every house had electric light and running water, with inside toilets and bathrooms. Indeed Scar folk were the envy of the local population, the majority of whose domestic arrangements were far less sophisticated. There was the school and a cinema and medical care was readily available in the well-staffed little hospital.

Above all this however, there was the place itself, a paradise of hills and streams and fresh air. What a place to grow up in. It is little wonder that those children of Scar come back here as often as they can, sometimes with others as members of the Scar Village Association, to talk and reminisce. Sometimes they come alone, to sit in quiet contemplation of the scene, seeing and hearing sights and sounds denied to the rest of us. I well remember one autumn visit. It was a beautiful crisp, clear October day, a day for Scar at its best. There was only one other car on the park when I drove in and I stood waiting at the end of the dam whilst an elderly lady took a photograph of her husband, the blue water and the russet hillside behind him. She turned and smiled at me. "You see," she said, as if by way of explanation, "my husband was born here."

Across on the far side of the reservoir lies the hamlet of Lodge. Now reduced to tumbled piles of stone, it was once the "metropolis" of the dale head. A meeting point of drove roads from the north and west, the little settlement got its name from the monastic lodge

Scar House reservoir from Lodge

which was once established here. If these stones could speak they would have many a story to tell and maybe shed some light on the mystery which surrounds a gruesome discovery on Dead Man's Hill. The parish record book at Middlesmoor records the event thus: "May 30th 1728. Three murder'd bodies were found buried on Lodge Edge without heads".

The true details of what happened here will never be known, but local tradition maintains that these were the bodies of three Scottish pedlars, murdered for their money or wares, whilst staying at Lodge. Tradition also has a culprit, one Margaret Thompson, who ran a boarding house at Lodge. Rumour and innuendo current at the time does in fact point in her direction, but as to whether she actually did the deed remains very much open to question. At the very least she must have had one accomplice, for the bodies had to be carried and buried in the peat on the hill top and why, if the victims were to be hidden in this way, go to the extreme of decapitating each one? I have heard an alternative explanation of the story, which suggests that the three bodies were sacrificial victims. Of course this would point to the events taking place very many hundreds of years before Margaret Thompson appeared on the scene, but the hill top location and the missing heads are quite characteristic of Celtic ritual practise. Whatever, the answer to all this lies buried in Middlesmoor churchyard and is likely to remain so.

The road from Scar to Angram follows the side of the reservoir, below the dark hillside scars which give the place its name. This side of the valley is almost always in shadow, for it faces due north. It was said that the sun never shone on Scar House farm during the winter – a bleak prospect indeed. Angram dam is like a smaller version of Scar, rising some one hundred and thirty feet above the river and holding back 1,100 million gallons of water. It has exactly half the capacity of its larger neighbour. With no cloaking plantation to soften its outline, Angram's gauntness matches well with the stark hills which surround it. From here the moorland sweeps up to the summit of Great Whernside. This is where the Nidd begins and our journey ends, home to the grey Swaledale sheep, where the silence is broken only by the harsh warning cry of the Red Grouse.

The Walks

Nidderdale now has its own dedicated Ordnance Survey map, number 26 in the 1;25,000 scale Explorer Series. This covers all but the eastern most part of the area, for which walkers will also require OS 1:25,000 Pathfinder Series maps 663 and664. Armed with these, Nidderdale is now your oyster.

The walks detailed are clearly shown on these maps and make use only of public rights of way and occasionally permissive paths where a right of way has been specially negotiated with the landowner. Be assured if you follow these walks you have every right to be there, but please remember many of them pass through cultivated or meadow land and some go through the middle of farmyards. Keep to the path and close all gates. As yet their is no "right to roam" over open moorland and of course a vast expanse of heather is not just a vast expanse of heather, it is grazing for sheep and a breeding ground for grouse. Heather moor is especially vulnerable in summer when a carelessly discarded cigarette may cause fire.

All the walks in the book are circular routes and vary in length from between 4 and 9 miles. Some are easy afternoon strolls and none of them are particularly difficult, though there are one or two steep climbs in places. They have been chosen to take in some of the most beautiful scenery and places of interest within the area and, where possible, are centred on, or close to places where refreshments are available.

Walk 1. Moor Monkton and the Red House

Distance: 4 miles (6.5 km)

Grade: Easy level walking.

Start and finish: Moor Monkton. Limited parking on the road at the eastern end of the village.

Things to see: The Nidd-Ouse confluence. Views of Nun Monkton and Benningborough Hall. The Red House chapel.

Refer to: Chapter 1

Maps: OS Pathfinder 664

❖ Walk to the end of the road and through the gate, keeping to the track which runs parallel to the river. Do not turn onto the track which leads to Laund House farm, but keep to the grassy path, *straight ahead.*

❖ Go through the gate and across the field to the river, then turn right along the riverbank.

❖ Pass over two stiles, through a double gate and past the water treatment works.

❖ On reaching the environs of the Red House do not go through the gate, but take the permissive path along the embankment top, which runs around the edge of the old moat. The path drops down to a footbridge, then rises to meet the road.

❖ At the road turn left if you wish to visit the Red House chapel, or turn right and walk along the road, past Park farm, for about 1 mile.

❖ Just before the isolated house you will see a track off to the right. Turn here, go through the gate and straight across the field to the woodland ahead.

❖ On reaching the woodland boundary turn left, along the edges of two fields, then follow the track around to the right to gate. Go through this and onto the grassy track, which will lead you back to Moor Monkton.

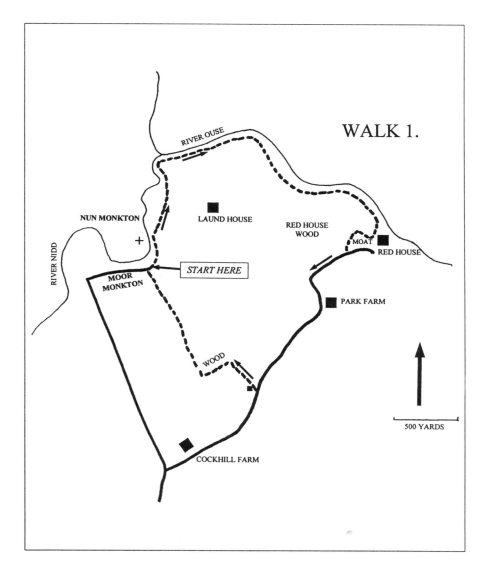

Walk 2. Tockwith

Distance: 6½ miles (10.5 km)

Grade: Easy level walking.

Start and finish: Tockwith. Parking on the road near the church.

Things to see: Good views along the river. A glimpse of the White Horse at Kilburn(on a clear day) and the site of a battle.

Refreshments: Two pubs in Tockwith.

Refer to: Chapter 1

Maps: OS Pathfinder 664

❖ Walk westward along the village street, past the church, following the road as it bends round to the right.

❖ About 200 yards beyond the bend turn right onto the signposted public bridleway.

❖ At the end of the second field on your left you will see a track off to the left. Turn here and follow this for about ½ mile to a gate and some new farm buildings.

❖ Do not go through the gate, but turn sharp right and follow the track round to a gate and stile.

❖ Go over the stile and across the field to the gate ahead. Go through this gate and straight across the field to a stile.

❖ Cross the stile and climb the embankment, turning right at the top to follow the river.

❖ Your way ahead follows the river bank over various stiles and eventually past the derelict remains of Skewkirk mill and, half a mile beyond that, Skewkirk Hall.

❖ Continue along the embankment and as you approach New farm you will come to a gate and stile. Cross the stile and follow the fence around to the left, through a rather woody patch of riverside, then over a stream just beyond the farm.

❖ Turn right along the stream side and then over the stile onto the track.

❖ Turn right, past the farm and join the public bridleway straight ahead.

As you approach the sharp right bend in the road you are now looking out across the famous battlefield of Marston Moor. Follow the road, bearing sharp left at the next corner, from where Kendal Lane will lead you back to Tockwith.

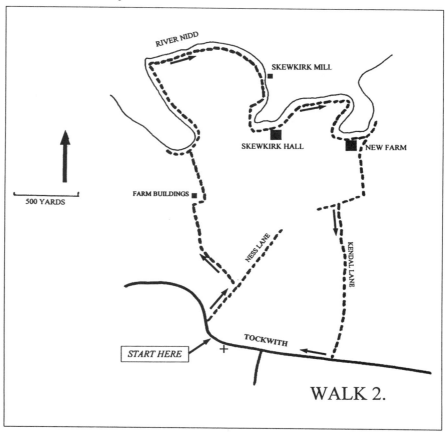

WALK 2.

Walk 3. Green Hammerton to Whixley

Distance: 4 miles (6.5 km)

Grade: Easy level walking, some of it along quiet by- roads.

Start and finish: The village green in Green Hammerton.

Things to see: Long distance views over open country, two Roman roads, Whixley church and the final resting place of Christopher Tancred (key required ask at the post office).

Refreshments: Pub in Whixley.

Refer to: Chapter 2

Maps: OS Pathfinder 664

❖ Walk along the road alongside the village green and onto the track straight ahead, signposted "public footpath to Thorpe Under-wood".

❖ Through the farmyard and bear right behind the sheds to follow waymarked path across the field.

❖ Walk straight ahead towards the patch of woodland on the far side of the field, then over a ditch and stile on the right-hand side of the wood.

❖ Continue with the woodland on your left and, where the wood-land ends, go through the gate and walk straight ahead with the hedge on your left.

❖ Cross the stream and go diagonally across the field to stile in the right-hand corner, then diagonally across the next field towards the corner of the wood.

❖ Cross the stream and turn left along the edge of the field, past the jumps and eventually out onto Thorpe Green Lane.

❖ Turn left and follow the road. In approximately one mile you will come to the junction with the B6265, the Roman road from York to Boroughbridge. Go straight across and in another quarter of a mile

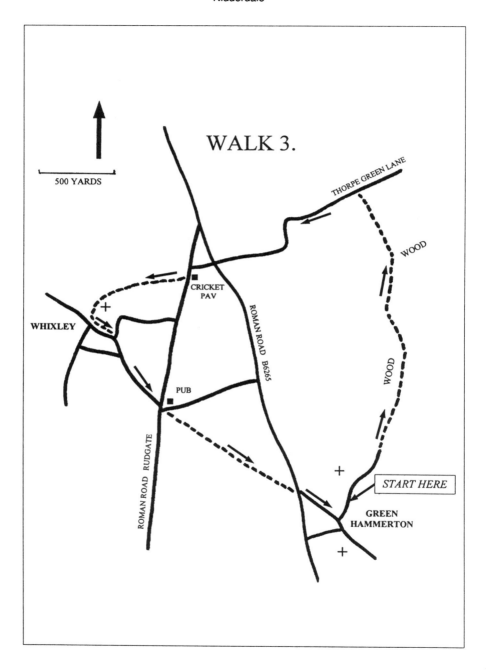

WALK 3.

500 YARDS

THORPE GREEN LANE

WOOD

WOOD

WOOD

CRICKET
PAV

WHIXLEY

ROMAN ROAD B6265

PUB

ROMAN ROAD RUDGATE

START HERE

GREEN
HAMMERTON

you will come to a junction with yet another Roman road, known as the Rudgate.

❖ Turn left and walk down the road to the gate opposite the cricket pavilion.

❖ Go through the gate and walk up the field side to the top of the rise, then diagonally across the next field, heading towards the top right-hand corner of the church yard.

❖ Walk down the narrow path alongside the church yard and out onto Church Lane.

❖ Turn left and walk along to the junction with the High Street, then right long High Street, across the road and to the pub.

❖ Across the road behind the pub is a gate and sign post pointing across the fields to Green Hammerton. Follow this diagonally across four fields, to come out just above the road junction. Bear left and follow the lane back into the village.

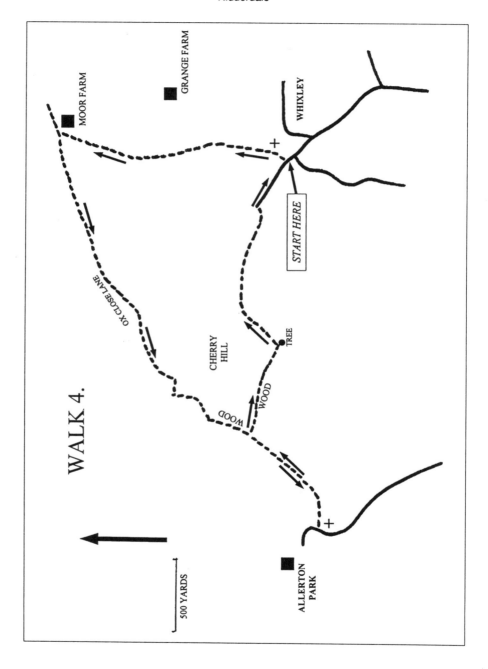

WALK 4.

500 YARDS

MOOR FARM

GRANGE FARM

OX CLOSE LANE

WHIXLEY

START HERE

CHERRY HILL

WOOD

WOOD

TREE

ALLERTON PARK

Walk 4. Whixley to Allerton Mauleverer

Distance: 5 miles (8 km)

Grade: Gentle walking through rolling countryside.

Start and finish: Near the church in Whixley.

Things to see: Whixley church and the final resting place of Christopher Tancred (key required — ask at the post office). Beautiful long distance views. An unusual church at Allerton (key required — see notice board) and the wonderful "gothic" house at Allerton Park, open to visitors Sundays and bank holidays from Easter until the end of September.

Refreshments: Pub in Whixley.

Refer to: Chapter 2

Maps: OS Pathfinder 664

❖ Take the narrow path, signposted "to Little Ouseburn" up the side of the church, through the gate at the top, then left through the gate in the adjacent fence.

❖ Once through the gate turn right and follow the hedgeline, looking out for the way markers as you go.

❖ In approximately ¾ mile the path veers away from the hedge to cut diagonally across four fields to the lane just by the entrance to Moor farm.

❖ Turn left along the lane and continue along straight ahead, past the junction with Starra Field Lane and onto Ox Close Lane.

❖ The track soon degenerates into a narrow path, which passes between tall overgrown hedges, to emerge at the corner of a large field.

❖ Walk ahead to the far end of the field and at the track junction turn right then sharp left to walk alongside the holly hedge.

❖ At the end of the field turn right and walk to the hedge straight ahead. When you reach it turn left and follow it round to the coni-fer plantation.

❖ Follow the track through the plantation, then along the edge to the cross-roads where the plantation ends.

❖ If you wish to visit Allerton Park and the church go straight across and follow the road into Allerton. You will then retrace your steps back to the cross-roads and turn right past the end of the planta-tion.

❖ The good surface soon deteriorates into a rutted track along the field edge. Continue ahead until you come to a large tree at the end of a field. Here the track bears round to the left. Follow this through some scrub at the end of the field, and then turn right onto a track, which soon meets a metalled farm road, which will lead you back into Whixley.

Walk 5. Goldsborough, Plompton and Ribston

Distance: 8½ miles (14 km)

Grade: Gentle walking through rolling countryside.

Start and finish: Near the church in Goldsborough.

Things to see: The pretty village of Goldsborough with its hall and church, Plompton Rocks and Ribston Hall, some good views of the river and fine long distance views over the surrounding countryside

Refreshments: Pub in Goldsborough.

Refer to: Chapter 3

Maps: OS Pathfinder 663

❖ From the church walk back up the village street and turn left down Midgely Lane and follow the bridle path between the duck pond and the new houses.

❖ When you reach Goldsborough Mill farm go through the farm-yard, across the bridge and up to the road.

❖ Cross the road and go through the gate opposite and through another gate in the far corner of the field.

❖ Cross the road (take care here) and follow the bridleway marker on the far side.

❖ At the top of the rise walk straight ahead between the hedge and the caravans and at the end of the metalled track go straight on through the wood.

❖ The path emerges at the road (same one! take care again) go across and follow the bridleway marker along the woodland edge.

❖ When you reach the end of the wood Plompton Hall can be seen straight ahead. Turn sharp right and follow the track towards the hall.

❖ Follow the diversion signed path to the right, which goes along the edge of the conifer plantation and down to a gate in the corner of a field.

❖ Go through the gate and diagonally across the field to another gate in the far corner.

❖ Through the gate and take the second path on the right (waymarked) which eventually leads to a gate into a field.

❖ Walk diagonally across the field to a gate opposite a road junction then follow the bridleway sign towards Plompton High Grange.

❖ Before entering the farmyard follow the detour sign around the buildings and onto the track towards Loxley farm.

❖ Pass to the right of Loxley farm following the track through the wood.

❖ On emerging from the wood follow the woodland edge then turn left past Throstle Nest farm.

❖ Beyond the farm the metalled road gives way to a rough grassy track, past a patch of woodland, then straight across three fields towards some houses straight ahead.

❖ At the end of the third field turn right and walk down the hedge side and through the gate to the road.

❖ Turn left into Little Ribston.

❖ At the junction turn right along the main road and in about ¼ mile turn left into South Park Lane.

❖ Pass behind the lodge and in front of the cottages, then through the gate and out into Ribston Park. Follow the road over the bridge and bear left following the waymarker.

❖ When you reach the buildings at the far end of the park look out for a waymarker on the left between the wooded area and the field. Go through the gate and onto the green lane, following the waymarkers. The path drops down towards the river, through High Wood, over a stream, then climbs gently to meet a broad track which will lead you back to Goldsborough.

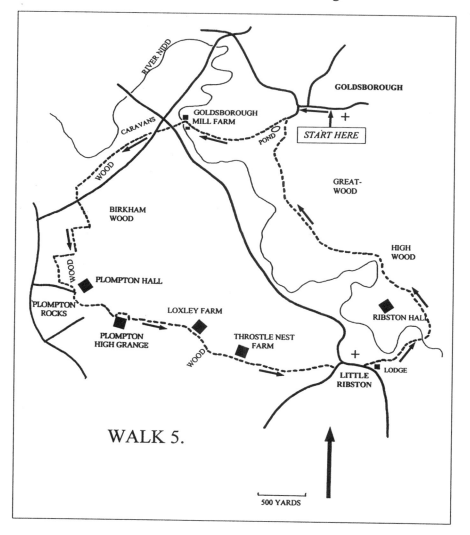

WALK 5.

500 YARDS

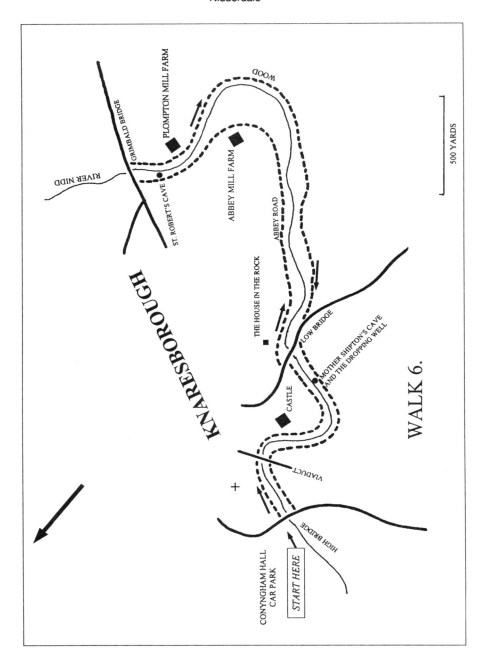

KNARESBOROUGH

WALK 6.

RIVER NIDD

GRIMBALD BRIDGE

PLOMPTON MILL FARM

ST. ROBERT'S CAVE

ABBEY MILL FARM

ABBEY ROAD

WOOD

THE HOUSE IN THE ROCK

LOW BRIDGE

MOTHER SHIPTON'S CAVE AND THE DROPPING WELL

CASTLE

VIADUCT

HIGH BRIDGE

CONYNGHAM HALL CAR PARK

START HERE

500 YARDS

Walk 6. Knaresborough Riverside

Distance: 4½ miles (7 km)

Grade: Gentle strolling, mainly on the level.

Start and finish: The High Bridge in Knaresborough.

Things to see: The viaduct. The Chapel of Our Lady in the Crag. The House in the Rock. St. Robert's Cave. The Dropping Well. Mother Shipton's Cave.

Refreshments: Pubs, cafés etc. in Knaresborough.

Refer to: Chapter 4

Maps: OS Pathfinder 663

❖ From the town end of the High Bridge turn into the narrow lane called Waterside.

❖ Walk past the boat landings and under the viaduct and continue along the road until you come to the Low Bridge.

❖ Go directly across the road here and into Abbey Road, where soon on the left you will see two of Knaresborough's greatest curiosities, the Chapel of Our Lady in the Crag and, above it, the House in the Rock.

❖ Having surveyed these two unique properties, continue along Abbey Road, where in about ¾ mile you will reach St. Robert's Cave and eventually emerge at Grimbald Bridge.

❖ Cross the bridge and immediately turn right along the riverbank, past the farm and the weir.

❖ The path follows the riverside through woodland and fields, eventually meeting the road just above the Low Bridge.

❖ Cross the road and walk down towards the bridge, where, just before the Mother Shipton Inn you will see the entrance to the Dropping Well Estate.

❖ Pay your toll, which also gives access to Mother Shipton's Cave and the Dropping Well, then continue through the woodland, to emerge once again at the High Bridge.

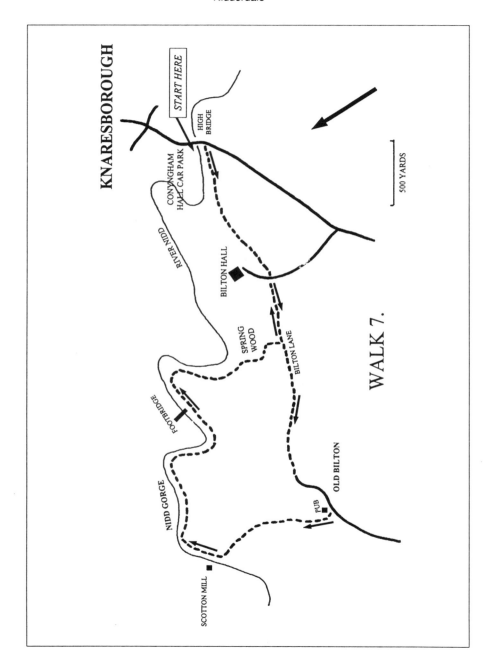

Walk 7. The Nidd Gorge

Distance: 6 miles (10 km)

Grade: A couple of steep descents and ascents into and out of the gorge and some muddy walking in the gorge in wet weather.

Start and finish: At the High Bridge in Knaresborough.

Things to see: Knaresborough, the wooded gorge, wild plants and animals.

Refreshments: Various pubs, hotels and restaurants in Knaresborough. Pub in Old Bilton.

Refer to: Chapters 4 and 5

Maps: OS. Pathfinder 663

❖ Turn left at the south side of the High Bridge onto the cycleway along the river, opposite Conyngham Hall car park.

❖ Leave the cycleway at the foot of the hill and take the waymarked footpath through the trees.

❖ Rejoin the cycleway at the top of the hill and turn right through the gate, continuing straight ahead towards Bilton Hall.

❖ Go straight across at the entrance to Bilton Hall, into Bilton Lane and follow it into the picturesque hamlet of Old Bilton.

❖ Just beyond the pub turn right into a lane signposted "to Nidd Gorge" and, just before the entrance to Woodside farm, turn right through the waymarked gate.

❖ Follow the path along the field side and between tall hedges, then down steeply into the wooded gorge.

❖ The path bears round to the right. Follow it but keep descending towards the river, where you will emerge opposite Scotton Mill.

❖ Turn right and follow the path, which closely borders the river through the gorge.

❖ After approximately 1 mile you will pass a footbridge. Do not cross the bridge but follow the path which soon turns away from the river and begins to climb steeply up to the right.

❖ Eventually the path levels out to run along the edge of the gorge, before turning away between two fields and issuing, via a gate, back out into Bilton Lane.

❖ Turn left and retrace your steps past Bilton Hall and back to the High Bridge.

Walk 8. Ripley to Burnt Yates

Distance: 8 miles (13 km)

Grade: Part of which follows the Nidderdale Way. Fairly easy walking with only one steep climb. The path can however be very muddy in places.

Start and finish: The car park at Ripley

Things to see: Ripley church and castle, Clint cross and stocks, Hampsthwaite village and church, Birstwith bridge, The New Brig, Burnt Yates School.

Refreshments: Cafés in Ripley and Hampsthwaite, Pubs in Ripley, Hampsthwaite, Birstwith and Burnt Yates.

Refer to: Chapter 5

Map: OS Explorer 26

❖ From the car park walk into the village square and along past the church and castle gates.

❖ Following Hollybank Lane, cross over the stream and continue along the broad track, which in about 1 mile comes out onto a metalled road. Continue along this to the road junction in Clint.

❖ Cross the road and immediately over a stile into a field. Keeping to the wall side walk down to the gate and out onto the road at the bottom, then forward over the bridge and into Hampsthwaite.

❖ Walk up the street and follow the road round to the right when you reach the village green and continue along the Birstwith road.

❖ In about ½mile you will come to an isolated barn at the roadside, immediately behind which is a gate and signpost to Birstwith.

❖ Cross the field and down to the river, which is now followed into Birstwith, following the signposted detour around Wreaks Mill before entering the village.

❖ Cross the road and, skirting the playing field, continue along the river bank for about ¾ mile to the New Brig.

❖ Go over the bridge and follow the old pack horse track steeply up-

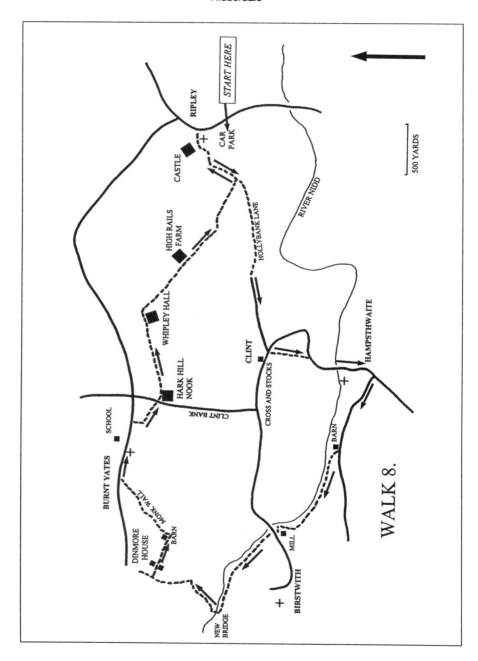

WALK 8.

hill to a point where the gradient levels out. In the field corner there is a stile which you cross and head straight towards the group of buildings which lie ahead.

❖ Leave the field by the gate and turn right down the road, between the two buildings and cross to the top left corner of the yard, where another gate leads out into a field.

❖ Walk ahead along the edge of the field and a patch of woodland, until you come to another gate with two way-marker arrows on it.

❖ Through the gate and follow the diagonal arrow up to the barn, where you cross into the next field.

❖ Turn up hill and walk up past the back of the barn and continuing with the wall on your left. This is the line of the old Monk Wall, which you follow right the way up to join the road at Burnt Yates.

❖ Cross the stile and turn right along the road into the village.

❖ Walk through the village and in about half a mile you will see a signposted stile on the right. Go over the stile and head diagonally across the field to the gate in the bottom corner.

❖ Go out onto the road and turn right, then almost immediately, before reaching the group of farm buildings, you will see a stile on the left. Cross the stile and follow the edge of the field keeping the wall to your right.

❖ At the end of the wall cross two stiles so that now the fence line is on your left. Head for the top corner of the wood you can see in the distance. From the wood you will see a group of farm buildings straight ahead. Make for these, following the detour through the gate in the hedge just before reaching the buildings.

❖ When you come out onto the road turn right, between the gate-posts and along the permissive track, past the farm buildings. Soon you will pick up the boundary wall of Ripley Park on your left, which you follow down to Hollybank Lane and then retrace your steps back to Ripley.

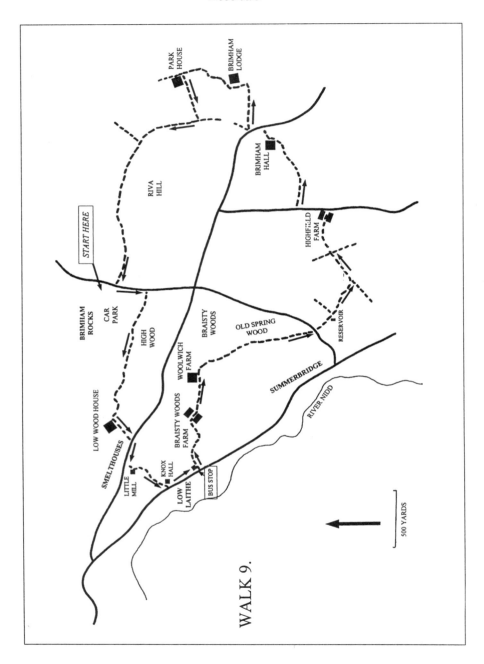

WALK 9.

Walk 9. The Hartwith Round – from Brimham Rocks

Distance: 8 miles (13 km)

Grade: Very varied walking, with just one steepish climb.

Start and finish: Brimham Rocks car park (NT parking charge sometimes)

Things to see: Brimham Rocks, moorland, woodland and farmland. Some beautiful views of the dale and lots of wild flowers in late spring. Some fine old farmhouses.

Refreshments: Café at Brimham Rocks, pub at Low Laithe, teas and snacks at the "Hiker's Rest" Brimham Lodge.

Refer to: Chapter 5

Maps: OS Explorer 26

❖ From the car park walk back to the road and turn right along the road for about ¼ mile before turning right onto a track signposted "to Smelthouses".

❖ Go through the wooden gate and into the wood, where the path becomes somewhat indistinct and boggy. Continue straight ahead with the wall on your right.

❖ After leaving the wood the path descends between walls towards Low Woodhouse farm.

❖ On reaching the farm go through the gate and out onto a metalled track. Turn left and walk down to the road.

❖ Turn right towards Smelthouses and continue along the road as far as the post box, where you turn left onto a bridleway, passing Little Mill, to walk alongside Fell beck.

❖ The track swings away from the beck to meet the main road where you turn left and walk along the footpath into the village of Low Laithe.

❖ Pass the pub (if possible), then immediately beyond the bus stop and telephone box turn left between the buildings, through the gate and steeply uphill through the woodland.

❖ At the top of the wood cross the stile and follow the wall side to Braisty Woods farm.

❖ Go through the gate and turn right between the farm buildings. At the first junction bear left, then right at the second junction following the signpost to Woolwich farm.

❖ When you reach Woolwich farm go straight ahead through the gates and past the barn.

❖ Leave the track and enter the wood at the gate adjacent to the corrugated iron shed.

❖ Follow the path through the wood straight ahead, through Old Spring Wood and eventually out to the road past a house and pond.

❖ Cross the road and go through the gate, walking straight ahead with the woodland above you to your left.

❖ When you pass the reservoir turn uphill to the gate and on up the steep rock path, to join a waymarked walled green lane, which continues to wind gently uphill to a gate and another green lane.

❖ Go across this lane and over the stile, straight ahead towards another stile at the far end of the field.

❖ Continue straight ahead across the next field then through the gate and along the track through the conifer plantation, to emerge onto the road through the farmyard at Highfield farm.

❖ Turn left and walk past the caravan site and in about 300 yards look out for a stile in the corner of the field on your right.

❖ Cross the stile and walk down the wall side to the end of the field, where you cross another stile and continue straight ahead downhill, bearing slightly to the left to reach a bridge and gate, which leads into the farmyard at Brimham Hall.

❖ Turn left through the farmyard, then right uphill to the road.

❖ Turn left along the road for about 200 yards then turn right following the Nidderdale Way signpost towards Brimham Lodge.

❖ Brimham Lodge is one of the oldest and finest farmhouses in the dale, you can see it quite clearly as you pass by, but for a better view call in for a cup of tea and a slice of home-made cake at the "Hiker's Rest".

❖ On leaving Brimham Lodge continue through the farmyard and down the winding track which leads to Park House. Turn left immediately in front of Park House and cross the field onto a track leading up to a gate at the corner of the wood.

❖ Go through the gate and straight ahead uphill to a stile.Cross the stile onto the lane and turn right. You are now back on the Nidderdale Way. Follow the waymarked route back to the car park at Brimham Rocks.

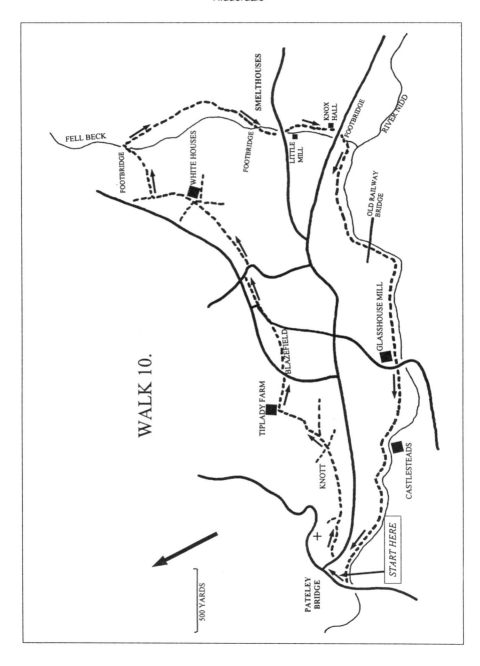

WALK 10.

Walk 10. Panorama Walk to Fellbeck and Glasshouses

Distance: 7 miles (11 km)

Grade: Very varied walking, easy going in most parts, but rough and often wet in others.

Start and finish: Pateley Bridge car park (parking charge)

Things to see: Some fine views of the dale. The wooded confines of Fell beck, full of bluebells in late spring and ending in a pleasant riverside stroll to Glasshouses mill and back to Pateley.

Refreshments: Cafés and pubs in Pateley, pub at Low Laithe, teas and snacks at the "Winery" Glasshouse mill.

Refer to: Chapter 6

Maps: OS Explorer 26

❖ From the car park in Pateley, walk up to the top of the High Street and turn right along Ripon Road.

❖ Turn left up the steps signposted "Panorama Walk" and follow the winding path uphill to the cemetery gates. From here you can walk up through the cemetery and visit the old church of St Mary's, retracing your steps to the gate to continue.

❖ You are on the Nidderdale Way. Walk ahead through the tiny hamlet of Knott.

❖ Turn up left through the gorse when you reach the signpost to Blazefield, crossing the field diagonally to the stile in the top corner.

❖ Cross the stile and go straight ahead to cross two more stiles and enter a green lane.

❖ Cross the lane and through the gate, bearing uphill to the left, towards the farm buildings ahead. Go through the gate and over the stream and up the track to another gate.

❖ Go through the gate into Tiplady farm, turning right to follow the farm track.

- ❖ When you reach the road cross and follow the Nidderdale Way which leads you along the front of the row of cottages and past a number of houses.
- ❖ On reaching the metalled road turn left uphill as far as the junction with a broad track, which leads off straight ahead.
- ❖ Go along the track which soon becomes very narrow and overgrown.
- ❖ Turn downhill when you reach the road and continue down until you reach the Nidderdale Way marker pointing along a track off to the left.
- ❖ Turn onto the track, which takes you through the hamlet of White Houses, then gently downhill.
- ❖ Just before you reach the next building turn sharp right following the waymarker, over the stile and down the wall side to another stile at the bottom of the field.
- ❖ Cross the stile and follow the waymarkers onto the track and over the cattle grid.
- ❖ Turn downhill to the right and follow the Nidderdale Way signs to the footbridge.
- ❖ Cross the bridge and turn sharp right to follow the path through the wood, signposted "Smelthouses".
- ❖ When you reach the derelict brick buildings turn down to the beck, cross the footbridge and continue downstream, eventually to emerge onto the road in Smelthouses.
- ❖ Turn left along the road, then right just before the post box, along the public bridleway, to reach the Pateley-Ripon road at Knox Manor.
- ❖ Cross the road and follow the signpost to Glasshouses, across the field and over the footbridge.
- ❖ A good broad track now leads along the riverside to Glasshouses, where it emerges into the mill yard. Time now to sample some country wines or have a cup of tea at the Winery, before crossing the road and following the footpath past the reservoir and back into Pateley.

Jenny Twigg and her daughter Tib

Middlesmoor church

The driveway to Bilton Hall in autumn

Gathering sheep at Angram

Nidd waterfall above Lofthouse

Walk 11. Greenhow, Hardcastle and Cockhill

Distance: 4 miles (6.5 km)

Grade: Mostly on good well-defined tracks.

Start and finish: At the Miners Arms in Greenhow.

Things to see: Beautiful long distance views over the moors and upper dale. The remains of Cockhill lead mines and smeltmill.

Refreshments: Pub in Greenhow.

Refer to: Chapter 7

Maps: OS Explorer 26

❖ From the pub carpark walk along the Pateley road, past the new graveyard and turn left down Cockhill Lane opposite the entrance to Coldstones quarry.

❖ Go through the gate (waymarked) onto the track to Coldstones farm and continue downhill past the farm. The track becomes grassy beyond the farm and eventually leads down to a narrow metalled road signposted "Nidderdale Way".

❖ Turn left past Low Hole Bottom, over the bridge and up the hill past Hillend.

❖ Continue along the track and over the bridge at Brandstone Dub.

❖ The track winds uphill above the beck and near the top of the rise meets another track coming in from the left.

❖ Turn left here over the stile and follow the narrow walled lane uphill to a clump of trees, where it joins another track.

❖ Turn left along this track, through the gate and follow it down into the remains of Gillfield and Cockhill mines.

❖ The track winds its way between the spoil heaps and ruins. You are heading for the gate just visible ahead on the skyline.

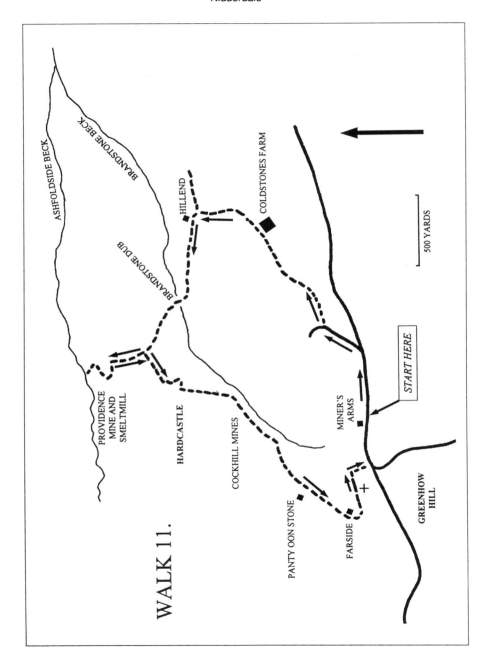

WALK 11.

ASHFOLDSIDE BECK

BRANDSTONE BECK

BRANDSTONE DUB

HILLEND

COLDSTONES FARM

500 YARDS

START HERE

PROVIDENCE MINE AND SMELTMILL

HARDCASTLE

COCKHILL MINES

MINER'S ARMS

PANTY OON STONE

FARSIDE

GREENHOW HILL

❖ Having explored the ruins (DO NOT ENTER ANY OF THE LEVELS) climb up to the gate and continue past Low Farside. If you look across the beck just above the buildings, you will see the Panty Oon stone.

❖ The track continues around Farside and comes out to meet the Pateley road just below the church.

Walk 12. Bewerley, Skrikes Wood and Guisecliff

Distance: 4½ miles (7 km)

Grade: Varied, including some road walking and often wet in the woodland.

Start and finish: By the green in Bewerley.

Things to see: Pretty Bewerley village and Bewerley Chapel, Skrikes Wood nature reserve, Yorke's Folly and the panoramic views of Nidderdale from Guisecliff.

Refreshments: None on route, but Pateley Bridge is nearby.

Refer to: Chapters 6 and 8

Maps: OS. Explorer 26

❖ From the village green walk back along the Pateley road to the junction opposite Bewerley farm and take the left-hand road past the farm.

❖ Just before the bridge over a stream a narrow gate in the wall leads into a field. Go through the gate and up the wall side then diagonally up hill across the next field to a gate on the skyline.

❖ From this gate the path leads down to an iron gate and into Fishpond wood.

❖ Take the (often muddy) path past the pond then follow the waymarker to bring you out onto the road.

❖ Turn right along the road and down to the bridge at Middle Tongue, where you turn left through the gate into Skrikes wood.

❖ Cross the footbridge, then at the track junction bear right and follow the winding path up hill through the wood.

❖ When you reach the Nidderdale Way sign turn right and continue on the broad track up through the wood, bearing left when you emerge from the woodland, to climb up, past an old quarry, to a stile in a high wall.

❖ Cross the stile and continue straight ahead along the path, which brings you to a gate and the road. Cross the road and follow the Guisecliff sign, heading for the twin columns of Yorke's Folly ahead on the skyline.

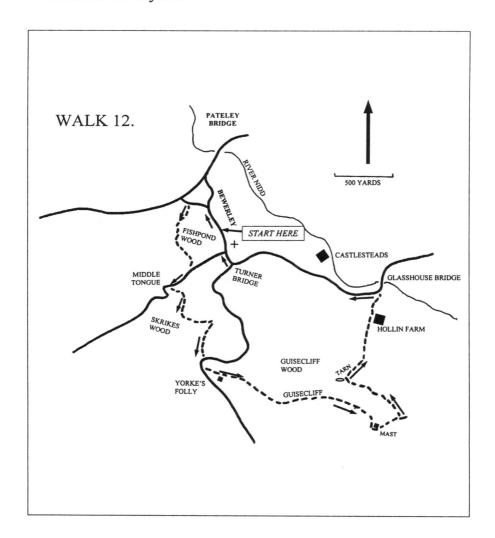

WALK 12.

PATELEY BRIDGE

RIVER NIDD

BEWERLEY

500 YARDS

FISHPOND WOOD

START HERE

CASTLESTEADS

MIDDLE TONGUE

TURNER BRIDGE

GLASSHOUSE BRIDGE

SKRIKES WOOD

HOLLIN FARM

GUISECLIFF WOOD

TARN

YORKE'S FOLLY

GUISECLIFF

MAST

❖ Your route now continues to follow the Nidderdale Way, along the top of Guisecliff, to the radio mast.

❖ Just beyond the mast leave the Nidderdale Way and turn down to the left over a high stile and follow the track which sweeps round to the left towards Guisecliff woods.

❖ Enter the wood on the broad track and follow it as it climbs gently upwards then sweeps back down to Guisecliff tarn.

❖ From the tarn take the rocky path down to the right to where it meets a broader track. Continue down hill to meet another track and turn left along it.

❖ At the next junction bear right down hill and almost immediately turn right down a narrow path which follows an old wire fence line.

❖ Keeping the old fence in view descend the often muddy path, which leads to a gap in a wall. Go through the gap, down the narrow path and out onto the track which leads to Glasshouses bridge. Do not cross the bridge, but turn left along the road which will take you past Castlesteads, Turner bridge and Bewerley Chapel and thence back into Bewerley.

Walk 13. Wath, Heathfield and Ashfoldside Beck

Distance: 5 miles (8 km)

Grade: Part of which follows the Nidderdale Way. Some steep climbs.

Start and finish: Pateley Bridge

Things to see: Pateley Bridge, lead mining remains

Refreshments: Cafés in Pateley. Pubs in Pateley and Wath.

Refer to: Chapters 7 and 8

Maps: OS Explorer 26

❖ The first part of the route, signposted "To Wath", just before the bridge, follows the line of the old Nidderdale Railway, through the meadows bordering the river and emerges into the hamlet of Wath just by the side of the bridge.

❖ Over the bridge and across the road, a signpost "to Heathfield" points steeply up the valley side. The path, which is not always very clear, slants diagonally across the hillside, running between a patch of woodland and a large solitary tree.

❖ The footpath passes through a gate in the wall at the top of the slope and eventually, by way of a detour around a farmyard, leads out onto the road and into the hamlet of Heathfield.

❖ Turn right along the road, past the little chapel, as far as the junction with a track which comes in diagonally from the left.

❖ A bridleway sign points off to the left along the track, which curves up to the brow of the hill. *Be sure not to follow the Nidderdale Way at this point.*

❖ From here the way is straight ahead, through a gate and down the wall side passing behind a field barn and towards Spring House Farm.

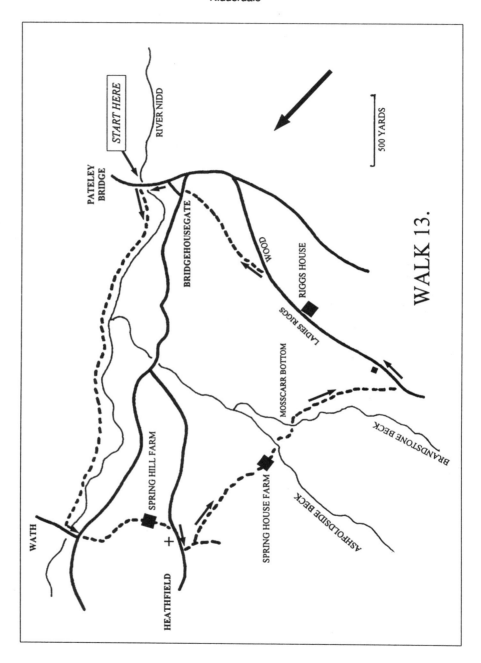

WALK 13.

START HERE

PATELEY BRIDGE

RIVER NIDD

BRIDGEHOUSEGATE

WOOD

RIGGS HOUSE

LADIES RIGGS

MOSSCARR BOTTOM

BRANDSTONE BECK

ASHFOLDSIDE BECK

SPRING HILL FARM

SPRING HOUSE FARM

WATH

HEATHFIELD

500 YARDS

❖ On reaching the last field before the farm leave the wall side and cut diagonally across the field and through the farmyard, leaving the yard by the right-hand metal gate.

❖ By following the hedge side it comes down to join the metalled road alongside Ashfoldside Beck.

❖ The way lies to the left along the road, past some caravans, as far as the new metal gate into the caravan site. Turn in at the gate and follow the track between the caravans and over the bridge.

❖ The track climbs quite steeply up the bank to the brow of the hill, from where a walled green lane (straight ahead) runs down to Mosscarr Bottom and to a footbridge over Brandstone Beck.

❖ Once over the bridge the path climbs steadily up the valley side, gradually rising higher above the beck.

❖ On reaching the metalled road turn left and follow it for about ¾ mile until it reaches the corner of a wood.

❖ Here a footpath goes off diagonally to the left, downhill across fields and eventually into Bridgehouse Gate.

❖ When you reach the road turn right, then in a couple of hundred yards, turn left onto the Pateley-Greenhow road, down over the bridge and back into Pateley.

Walk 14. The Gouthwaite Round

Distance: 7 miles (11 km)

Grade: Mostly pleasant easy strolling. Half of it on tarmac, but hopefully not too much traffic.

Start and finish: Wath bridge.

Things to see: Wildfowl and some lovely views over Gouthwaite reservoir.

Refreshments: Pubs in Wath and Ramsgill.

Refer to: Chapters 6 and 8

Maps: OS Explorer 26

❖ Cross the stile at the end of Wath bridge and follow the riverbank upstream.

❖ Cross a second stile, go across the field and into the woodland that encloses Gouthwaite dam.

❖ The path emerges at gate. Go through the opposite gate, across the first field, then diagonally uphill to join a well-defined track.

❖ Turn left long the track and follow it along the reservoir side, past Covill House farm and eventually out onto the road at Bouthwaite.

❖ Turn left, first crossing Lul beck, then left again over the Nidd and into Ramsgill.

❖ The route now follows the road, through the village and along the side of the reservoir.

❖ In approximately 2 miles you will pass Gouthwaite Hall and about 150 yards beyond there is a gateway and cattle grid on the right. Turn up here and follow the winding road uphill, through a patch of woodland and into the hamlet of Heathfield.

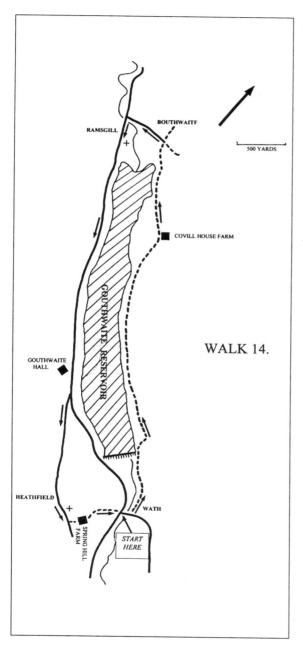

RAMSGILL

BOUTHWAITE

500 YARDS

COVILL HOUSE FARM

GOUTHWAITE RESERVOIR

WALK 14.

GOUTHWAITE HALL

HEATHFIELD

SPRING HILL FARM

WATH

START HERE

❖ Follow the road through the settlement and about 100 yards past the little chapel turn in along the drive to Spring Hill farm.

❖ Go directly across the farmyard to a gate and straight across the field to a stile.

❖ Over the stile and walk diagonally across the field, between the woodland and the tree. The path goes straight across the next field and over the stile to emerge opposite Wath bridge, from where you started.

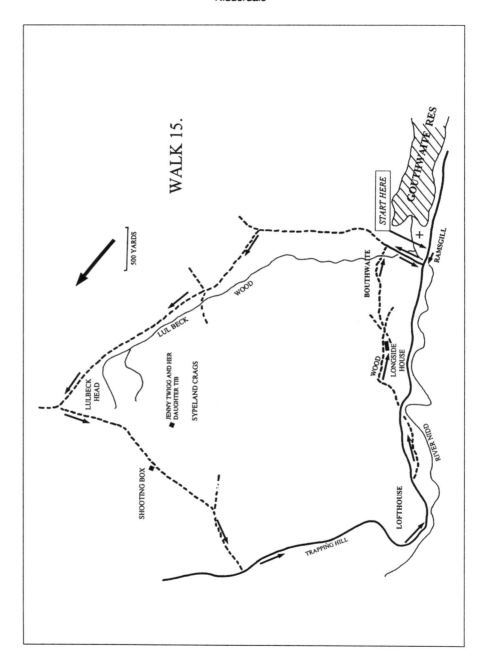

WALK 15.

500 YARDS

GOUTHWAITE RES

START HERE

RAMSGILL

BOUTHWAITE

WOOD

LUL BECK

LULBECK
HEAD

WOOD

LONGSIDE
HOUSE

JENNY TWIGG AND HER
DAUGHTER TIB

SYPELAND CRAGS

RIVER NIDD

SHOOTING BOX

LOFTHOUSE

TRAPPING HILL

Walk 15. Fountains Earth Moor

Distance: 9 miles (15 km)

Grade: One steep climb near the start, but mainly gentle walking on well-defined tracks and the road.

Start and finish: Ramsgill.

Things to see: Ramsgill village and church. Good views up and down the dale. The open, heather-clad moorland and weird rock formations of Sypeland Crags and Jenny Twigg.

Refreshments: Hotel in Ramsgill. Pub and Post Office in Lofthouse.

Refer to: Chapter 8

Maps: OS Explorer 26

❖ From the village green in Ramsgill, turn right along the road and over the bridge, then sharp right along the road to Bouthwaite.

❖ Where the road ends go straight ahead onto the track and through the gate.

❖ From here the track rises steeply up the hillside and eventually leads out onto the moorland.

❖ Turn left when you reach the "Unsuitable for Motor Vehicles" sign and continue along a good track past the top of the conifer plantation.

❖ When you arrive at the two gates go through the one straight ahead and along the gently rising track towards the skyline.

❖ Look out for the little boundary stone then a little farther on turn left at the junction.

❖ Your way now lies straight ahead, past the shooting house (look to your left beyond the shooting house to get good views of Jenny Twigg and her daughter) and eventually out to the tarmacked road, where you turn left and downhill into Lofthouse.

❖ Walk through the village and down to the main road. Turn left along the road and follow it as far as the "Nidderdale Way" marker pointing into the field on your right.

❖ Turn into the field, then left along a poorly defined path through the meadows, crossing the stiles and following the yellow waymarkers.

❖ When you reach the road, cross and rejoin the path which climbs steadily up the hillside towards the bottom edge of the conifer plantation ahead.

❖ The route follows the edge of the woodland, past Longside House, then down to meet a farm track at a gate.

❖ Go through the gate and along the track towards the cottage, but note that the right of way passes through the gate above the cottage and then on to a high ladder stile and gate.

❖ Cross the stile and continue ahead until you reach another stile. Cross here and walk down the field edge and over the bridge into Bouthwaite.Walk through the farmyard and onto the road which will take you back to Ramsgill.

Walk 16. Howstean Gorge, Blayshaw Gill and Stean

Distance: 3 miles (5 km)

Grade: Varied, but rough and often wet in places.

Start and finish: The car park at Howstean Gorge café.

Things to see: This walk may be combined with a visit to Howstean gorge, for which an entrance fee is payable. Other things to see include the ravine of Blayshaw gill and some panoramic views of the upper dale.

Refreshments: Available all day and in great variety at Howstean Gorge café.

Refer to: Chapter 8

Maps: OS Explorer 26

❖ From the car park turn left and walk back down the road to Studfold.

❖ Turn right along the road just before the entrance to the caravan park and right again up hill at the Nidderdale Way sign.

❖ Walk uphill past the cottages, then turn left along the track signposted "Ramsgill".

❖ A bridge carries the track over the deep ravine of Blayshaw gill, then at the top of the rise leave the Nidderdale Way to go right uphill on the track to High Blayshaw farm.

❖ The track goes past the front of the farm and rises to a gate.

❖ Go through the gate and along the wall side through two fields, then across a third field heading towards the conifer plantation and a gate in the far corner of the field.

❖ Go through the gate and along the fence line to a gate, from where you cross the next field diagonally uphill to a stile.

❖ Over the stile and down to the beck. You will need to find a suit-

Nidderdale

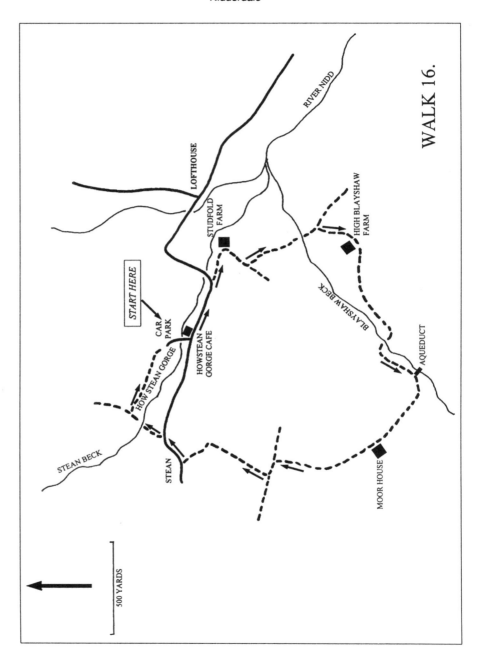

WALK 16.

able place to cross the beck and continue upstream as far as the aqueduct. The OS map is not too clear here as new planting and fences have been put in recently. However if you walk up the side of the aqueduct you will come to a wooden stile into the field.

❖ Cross the stile and follow the field wall along to where it emerges onto a track leading ahead towards Moor House farm.

❖ Enter the confines of Moor House farm by the gate and exit by the gate on the right. Turn sharp left along the track which leads to a gate and stile.

❖ Cross the stile and then go diagonally down hill, through a series of gates and stiles to emerge eventually on a track.

❖ Turn right then first left, then right at the next track junction, where this will lead you down hill into the little hamlet of Stean.

❖ Follow the winding road down through Stean, past the little green and seat, to where a Nidderdale Way sign points over a stile and into a field with a caravan.

❖ Cross the stile and follow the footpath down to the footbridge and up to a gate on the far side.

❖ Go across the field to the well-marked gap in the wall, then, ignoring the "Nidderdale Way" sign, walk straight across the field to the lower of the two gates.

❖ Walk through the next two fields by way of the waymarked gates to reach the barn, where you turn down right to the final gate and out into the car park from where you started.

Walk 17. Thrope Lane and Dale Edge

Distance: 6 miles (10 km)

Grade: Mostly on good well-defined tracks, some of them rather stony. One steep climb.

Start and finish: In the car park at Lofthouse.

Things to see: Pastoral views of the upper dale and the dry bed of the Nidd. Wonderful vistas of the dale head and beyond from Dale Edge.

Refreshments: Pub and shop in Lofthouse. Tea, coffee etc. at Thwaite House.

Refer to: Chapters 8 and 9

Maps: OS Explorer 26

❖ Turn right out of the car park in Lofthouse and walk up the road through the village and out onto the moorland road, which leads to Masham.

❖ Turn left onto the track signposted "Nidderdale Way" and go through the gate ahead. You are now on Thrope Lane, which you follow past Thrope farm.

❖ Beyond Thrope the track degenerates into a rough path, which drops steadily down to the river bed at Dry Wath.

❖ Cross here and go through the gate, following the path above the river bed, which, by way of two stiles eventually leads out into the environs of Limley farm.

❖ Walk through the middle of the farm yard, following the waymarkers, around the back of the buildings and onto a path which takes you down once again to the river bed.

❖ Cross the river bed and go through the gate uphill.

❖ The path winds its way uphill to Thwaite, where you enter by a gate. This is a good place to stop for a well-earned "cuppa" and to admire the view.

❖ Leave Thwaite by the waymarked gate and continue along a good track to Bracken Ridge.

❖ About 100 yards beyond the farm turn sharp right onto a track which rises steadily uphill onto the moor.

❖ At the top of the rise go through the gate and along the track, which hugs the dale edge, past the shooting house and eventually out to the Masham road above Lofthouse. Turn right downhill and back to the village.

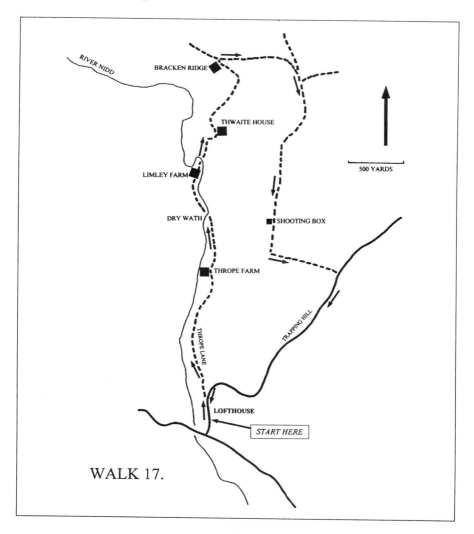

WALK 17.

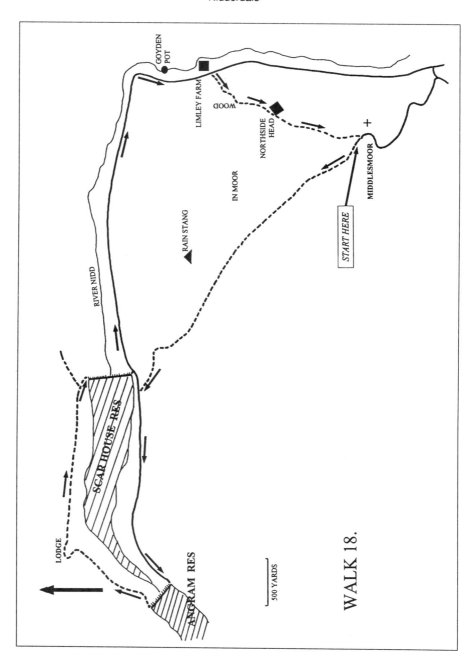

WALK 18.

500 YARDS

Walk 18. Middlesmoor to Scar House and Angram

Distance: 9 miles (14.5 km)

Grade: One steep down and one steep up, but mainly gentle walking on well-defined tracks and the road.

Start and finish: Middlesmoor.

Things to see: Middlesmoor village and church. Some dramatic views of the dale head. Scar House and Angram reservoirs. The massive sink hole of Goyden Pot.

Refreshments: Pub and teashop in Middlesmoor. Teas at Scar (sometimes)

Refer to: Chapters 8 and 9

Maps: OS Explorer 26

❖ From the car park in Middlesmoor turn right uphill and follow the track over In Moor and down to the shore of Scar House reservoir.

❖ Turn left, following the road along the side of the reservoir as far as Angram dam.

❖ Cross the dam and, either follow the permissive path along the northern shore of Scar House reservoir, or climb a little higher to walk through the ruins of Lodge hamlet, following the old lane back to Scar House dam.

❖ Cross the dam and turn left along the road.

❖ Follow the road for about 2½ miles, past the old railway tunnel, then look out on your left down to the river bed and Goyden Pot. A not too clear path leads down to the pot and returns to join the road at a gate in the top corner of the field.

❖ Continue along the road as far as Limley farm and go through the stile opposite the farmyard and steeply up hill, through the fields, towards the left-hand corner of the woodland, to join a farm track.

❖ Turn left through the gate and along the track past Northside Head farm. About 100 yards beyond the farm a stile leads into the field on the left, from where the path will take you back into Middlesmoor.

Also of Interest

WALKS IN THE MYSTERIOUS YORKSHIRE DALES

Graham Dugdale

A new approach to walking in this popular region, with 30 routes which unravel the many varied mysteries of the Yorkshire Dales. These tales dig deep into the region's history and folklore — follow in the macabre footsteps of the Swaledale corpse bearers, challenge the Penhill Giant in his own domain and listen for ghostly revelry at Ribblehead. £6.95

WEST YORKS WALKS: KIRKLEES

Martin Brewis

Walks in "Last of The Summer Wine" country — 26 circular walks range from 2½ to 7 miles and will help you discover the diverse beauty of the Kirklees area of West Yorkshire. From the secluded towns and villages in the Holme, Colne and Spen valleys to spectacular panoramic views from high ridges, there's a walk to grab everyone's imagination. £6.95

WEST YORKS WALKS: CALDERDALE & BRADFORD

Martin Brewis

26 circular walks which explore the dramatic landscape of Calderdale and Bradford. Surprisingly this includes rolling Pennine moorland, secluded dales, deans and cloughs and farming villages around Todmorden, Sowerby and Hebden Bridge, Haworth and Ilkley. Detailed routes are complemented by 'points of interest' for the inquisitive walker.

£6.95

BEST TEA SHOP WALKS IN WEST YORKSHIRE
Norman & June Buckley

A further volume in the now well-established tea shop walks series, covering part of the South Pennine area of first-class walking country, linked with selected tea shops in the towns and villages.

Easy-going walks are complemented by enjoyable and unusual tea shops en route. Full descriptions are given of the tempting delicacies that await the hungry walker. £6.95

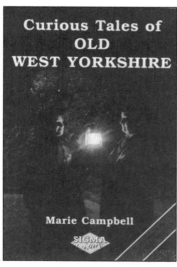

CURIOUS TALES OF OLD WEST YORKSHIRE
Marie Campbell

All things connected with the strange side to West Yorkshire's heritage are included: battles hard-fought upon the bleak moors, ancient folklore, superstitious practices and the witchcraft and wizardry of the Old Faith.

"In this fascinating, entertaining, bustling ... package of oddities, Marie Campbell ranges far and wide." BRADFORD TELEGRAPH & ARGUS £7.95

All of our books are available through booksellers. In case of difficulty, or for a free catalogue, please contact: **SIGMA LEISURE, 1 SOUTH OAK LANE, WILMSLOW, CHESHIRE SK9 6AR.**
Phone: 01625-531035   Fax: 01625-536800. E-mail: info@sigmapress.co.uk
Web site: http//www.sigmapress.co.uk
MASTERCARD and VISA orders welcome.